REVISED EDITION

2001 Household Hints and Dollar Stretchers

By Michael Gore

Completely revised, and with new material added, by the J. G. Ferguson Publishing Company, a division of Doubleday & Company, Inc.

J. G. FERGUSON PUBLISHING COMPANY
Chicago, Illinois
Distributed to the book trade by
DOUBLEDAY & COMPANY, INC.

ISBN: 0-89434-003-4
Library of Congress Catalog Card Number 76–57555

Contents

1

Your Meat Dollar

LISTEN TO THE ADVICE OF BUTCHERS AND PRIZE-WINNING COOKS—KNOW YOUR MEATS AND SAVE!

Variety is the spice of life. When shopping for meat remember that variety can add appetizing surprises to menus, extra value to your meat dollar. Save money by knowing the different, lower-cost cuts which can turn out as well as higher-cost cuts when prepared with imagination and care. Because of the constant changes in supply and demand, one cut may be the best buy one day, while a different one may be a "special" another day. A "special" usually means that a particular cut is more plentiful on the day offered. The lower price helps to keep meat moving while it is fresh. Remember, there are many, many meat cuts from which to choose.

ECONOMY IS OFTEN A QUESTION OF QUANTITY

Have at your fingertips some waste-preventing general rules as to how much meat to buy per serving. This is no problem, of course, when you buy chops or frankfurters: You simply count noses. But other meats require a bit of estimating. Here is a good general guide:

Boneless meat: ⅓ to ½ pound per serving of cutlets, stew meats, ground meat, rolled roasts, boneless round steak, etc. (Steaks for broiling, incidentally, should be one to two inches thick.)

Meat with average amount of bone: ½ pound per serving of bone-in roasts, steaks, ham, etc.

Meat with larger amount of bone: ⅔ to ¾ pound per serving of short ribs, spareribs, pork hocks, etc.

Another way to save is to buy quantity. That is, buy larger cuts. The butcher's "specials" quite often are found among the larger cuts. If your family is not large enough to require that amount of meat at a single meal, you have perhaps felt that these otherwise excellent buys would mean too many meals of the same kind. But there are various ways to get around that.

You don't have to prepare the whole cut at once. You can divide a larger cut into several really different meals. You can do the cutting yourself, in most cases, but your butcher is usually more than willing to oblige. Tell him how you want your meat cut.

NEW WAYS TO VARY
MEAT COURSE

For variety: variety meats. Liver, tongue, kidney, heart, brains, sweetbreads, tripe give your meat meals new flavor, often at sizable savings. Variety meats are rich in vitamins and minerals and delicious when prepared in such taste-tempting ways as these:

From the ground meats you can make wonderful treats, such as stuffed peppers, stuffed cabbage, meat loaf, Swedish meat balls, quick beef hash, turnovers, chili, beef drumsticks, and many of your own special recipes.

Inexpensive meat is coaxed to make gourmet pot roast by the foil-roasting method. This pot roast is not the result of water-braising, but of broiling and baking. The meat, placed on heavy aluminum foil, is first broiled by itself until brown, then turned for second-side browning. Add small onions and other taste-giving vegetables and pull up foil so that meat and vegetables are sealed into an airtight package. Then bake in very slow (300° F.) oven for 3 hours or more. Use no water. The meat and vegetables are "stewing in their own juice," since no liquid can evaporate. But for extra flavor you may add ¼ cup of red wine before sealing and baking.

Easiest way to cook bacon, if you're in no hurry, is in a low-temperature oven. Place strips of bacon on rack in a shallow roasting pan. Cook at 300–325° F. for an hour or more without bacon drying out or scorching. If you want to rush it, raise temperature to 375° F. and cook for ½ hour. This method requires no watching, turning, or other bother. Simply set a timer clock to remind you when the bacon is ready to serve.

Meat extenders make meat loaf and shopping dollar go further. Double size of meat loaf with soybeans, bread, cracker crumbs, or crushed dry cereal. Interesting idea: stuff meat loaf with the same kind of savory mixture you put into a roast chicken.

HOW TO BE A GENIUS
WITH LEFTOVERS

Dressed-up leftovers are fun to prepare, fun to eat. They tax the imagination but not the budget.

Leftover roast ends up in hash. But if a small amount of the hash is left over, use it hot as a filler for sandwiches made from well-browned French toast.

New idea for roast-beef bits. Everybody knows about using leftover roast-beef bits in sandwiches and combinations with vegetables in casserole, but here's a new trick: add them to canned chili for a hearty, different, luncheon main dish.

Miniature art. Grind leftover beef roast with a small onion. Store in a small covered dish in your refrigerator for several days. Let the family forget all about it, then spring it on them as midget meat loaves.

Meat-and-mushroom muffins. A small amount of leftover cooked beef may be ground and added to any standard muffin mixture. Serve the meat muffins hot, topped with a quick sauce made from undiluted mushroom soup.

Saucy meat loaf. Leftover meat loaf will seem new and different served the second time if topped with a tasty sauce. For instance, combine 2 cups applesauce, 2 tablespoons dry mustard with horseradish, 2 tablespoons Worcestershire sauce, and 3 tablespoons tomato catsup. Serve hot or cold on slices of the reheated loaf.

Three hard or soft rolls may be used as the basis of a luncheon dish. Scoop out center crumbs after splitting rolls, and save for any crumbing use. Fill the shells with any mixture of leftover meat or fish fixed with a little chopped celery and mayonnaise. Put in 350° F. oven until piping hot and lightly toasted, 25 to 30 minutes.

Part of a can of luncheon meat and leftover mashed white or sweet potatoes may be combined for a savory meat loaf. Slice the meat thin and sandwich it with the potato, mixed with a little mayonnaise. Bake at 350° F. until very hot and lightly browned, about 20 to 25 minutes.

Your stock goes up with meat stock used as the liquid in gelatins for molded meat loaves and aspics.

Don't pour flavor down the sink. Bacon drippings used for frying and for searing meat give it a fine, delicate flavor. But be sure to use a little less salt when you cook with bacon fat.

Additional ways with bacon drippings. Use it as shortening for bran muffins; to make white sauce, onion sauce, tomato sauce; in bread stuffing for veal, poultry, fish; as blend in some vegetables and soups; in bread crumbs or cereals to top vegetable or fish casseroles; to flavor macaroni, noodles, spaghetti; to grease muffin pans, to fry eggs, for flavor and economy; to brown croutons; to add to meat loaves. For shortening, strain through three thicknesses of cheesecloth.

TIPS ON PREPARING MEATS

Labor- and flavor-saving device. Line the broiler pan with aluminum foil and you do away with the scouring after broiling. The foil is non-inflammable and will catch melted fats that drip. Placing steak directly on aluminum foil, whose sides have been folded to stand up and form a very shallow foil pan, will leave broiler pan clean and will help seal in flavor and juice of steak. The melted steak fats and drippings are caught and can be used on the finished steak for extra juiciness.

Frozen meats may be roasted without thawing, but you must allow about one and one half the usual cooking time. Thawed meats are roasted same length of time as fresh meats.

Frying bacon faster. Frying time can be cut down, and more cooked at once, if you crisscross the slices and turn them all at once with a pancake turner.

Have hamburgers whenever you want them. Prepare them well in advance by shaping ground meat into patties and freezing. Wrap individually, or pack several together, separating each patty with double thickness of moisture-vaporproof material. Can be broiled without thawing, though it's necessary to allow more cooking time than for thawed patties.

Everybody's hamburger will be the same size if you measure meat with an ice-cream scoop. Scoop is ideal for this purpose and is easy to clean.

Keep lumps out of brown gravy. Add liquid slowly,

stirring and scraping with spoon. If there are lumps, strain gravy through sieve and reheat.

Using hot water often makes gravy lumpy. You may do better with cold water. A lumpless way to thicken gravy, and use cold water, is to have the water in a jar, adding flour and shaking until smooth, then adding to the meat liquids.

2

Poultry

ECONOMY HINTS AND COOKING METHODS FOR MORE VARIETY AND ENJOYMENT FROM DIFFERENT POULTRY

Checking on chickens. The chickens you buy at your local market are ready-to-cook. "Ready-to-cook" chickens are priced after head, feet, and viscera have been discarded. All poultry that moves in interstate commerce is subject to federal inspection to insure wholesome quality.

Chickens should be plump and youthful-looking. When buying chickens there are a number of quality controls you can exercise. Look at the drumstick. Don't buy if the chicken's thigh is thin and the bone heavy. Look at the neck. If it is well fleshed, the rest of the bird will probably be the same. Be careful if it has a long, scrawny neck, though. White, blue-tinged skin is not the mark of aristocracy in a chicken. The best meat chickens have creamy or light yellow skin.

HOW MUCH POULTRY TO BUY

When shopping for poultry, allow approximately ½ to 1 pound ready-to-cook bird per person, depending on how the chicken is to be served—which in turn

depends on how much other food you are planning to
serve with the chicken.

Larger birds may mean economy. These are called
fowl, hens, or stewing chicken. Their meat is less tender than that of smaller birds, but they are delicious
when slow-cooked in moisture and used in stew, fricas-
see with dumplings, chicken pies, or chicken à la king.

Better buy turkey. Because in larger birds there is
less bone in proportion to meat than in smaller birds,
turkey often is a better buy than chicken.

The "new look" in turkeys. Some years ago a new
style of turkey was developed, a new breed of broad-
breasted bird that gives you more white meat, less bone
waste with each turkey as compared with traditional
turkeys. The Beltsville turkey is one of these new birds.
It's a junior-size four-to-nine-pound turkey that suits
the needs of the small family of three to six people.

FROZEN POULTRY

Several good brands of frozen poultry are available.
You may buy whole-chicken broilers, fryers, roasters,
Rock Cornish game hens, stewing chickens, assort-
ments of chicken breasts, legs, thighs, wings, chicken
livers, giblets, hearts, gizzards—all cleaned and ready
to cook, after thawing. You can buy frozen young hen
turkeys, young tom turkeys, junior turkeys, Long Is-
land ducklings, and whole frozen capons that weigh
about four pounds or over. The capons are castrated
male birds that have a large proportion of white meat
and are packaged and prepared to be eaten as roasters.

Thaw frozen poultry completely before cooking.
There are three ways to do this:

1. Place poultry in its original wrapper or box in the
regular compartment of your refrigerator for about five
to six hours for every pound of bird. (Overnight for a
chicken, two to three days for a large turkey.)

2. For quicker thawing, place whole birds in cool

running water until just pliable enough to handle. This requires one to three hours. Do not allow to stand in water after thawing.

3. Packages of cut-up chicken or parts should be opened and contents placed on a rack in a shallow pan or tray until pieces can be separated. An electric fan, directed toward the thawing chicken, speeds the process.

To keep it from spoiling—keep poultry frozen in frozen-food compartment of your refrigerator until you plan to thaw and cook it.

Fry-'n-Freeze. While most fried foods should not be frozen for later use, fried chicken may be, if properly wrapped in moistureproof, vaporproof paper. May be eaten thawed out and cold at picnics, or from lunch boxes.

TIPS FOR ENJOYING POULTRY

Why not experiment with herbs? An easy trick is to tie together several large sprigs of parsley, a small sprig of tarragon, and one of thyme. Then drop this bouquet into a kettle of soup or stew, in fact add it to any meat or fowl dish that is cooked by moist heat. Or try putting an herb bouquet into the cavity of a roasting chicken. It does wonderful flavor things to the meat and eliminates the need for stuffing the chicken.

Use a cigarette lighter to singe pinfeathers left on dressed poultry. Result is neater, safer, quicker, and singeing that doesn't smudge the skin of the fowl.

Place a cored apple inside a roast chicken to keep meat moist and to add piquancy to flavor.

Decorating Christmas turkeys. Fringe two pieces of white or pink tissue paper or aluminum foil and wrap unfringed part around end of bird's legs. Foil will remain in place. Fasten paper fringe with fine thread of matching color.

If turkey is too large for your platter, wrap a tray with aluminum foil and use it for serving.

If leftover turkey is too big for your refrigerator, disjoint it, wrap loosely, and refrigerate.

Cover leftover refrigerated chicken. Its delicate flavor is lost and absorbs other food flavors easily. Don't try to keep cooked poultry more than a few days. Use it up as soon as possible in interesting leftover dishes, or wrap and freeze it.

Use stewed chicken in casserole specials, in pies, salads, sandwiches, chicken shortcakes, à la king, Tetrazzini, chicken loaf, with gravies, etc.

DON'T RISK FOOD POISONING

Stuff bird just before roasting. Don't stuff ahead of time, not even if you are going to refrigerate or freeze it.

Scoop out leftover stuffing from a leftover roast chicken or turkey and refrigerate each separately, in covered dishes or wrapped in waxed paper or aluminum foil. Stuffing should be used within two days. Fowl may be kept four to five days or longer if properly wrapped and frozen.

Never stuff a chicken or turkey with warm stuffing, then hold overnight before roasting.

Never let gravy, dressing, or cooked poultry stand at room temperature for even a few hours. Refrigerate them right after finishing the meal.

Never partially roast a large turkey one day, then leave it out of the refrigerator overnight to be completed the following day. If need be, get up early and put it in the oven before breakfast if you want to serve it at noon.

3

Carve Like a Connoisseur

IT'S AN ART, BUT HERE ARE THE ABC'S THAT MAKE IT SIMPLE

Carving skillfully takes a little practice, but it's neither tricky nor hard. And it's worth a little practicing, because when a perfectly cooked meat is properly carved, it is served at its appetizing best.

A sharp knife is the first requisite of good carving. Forged carbon steel makes the best, sharpest knife blades, according to chefs and gourmets, but many people prefer good-quality stainless steel because of its easier upkeep. Stainless steel blades do not rust (carbon steel knives must be dried immediately after being washed *because they do rust*) and they rarely need sharpening. Carbon steel blades, when sharp, are sharper than stainless blades, but should be sharpened each time they're used. Sharpen them on a "steel"— a rod of rough-surfaced steel fitted into a handle.

Carving a standing rib roast. It is best to have the backbone loosened by the butcher and then removed in the kitchen after roasting. Use a large carving knife. Set the roast on the platter as illustrated, rib bones to the left, large end away from carver. Insert fork, guard

up, between two top rib bones. Cut slices from outer
fat edge to bones, making slices no thicker than ¼
inch.

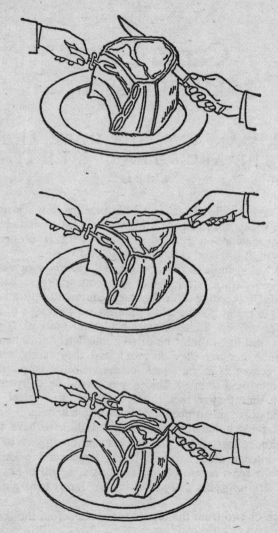

Free each slice by running the point of a knife along the edge where the meat joins the bone, and lift each slice off before starting the next. When you have sliced below the first bone, free it from the roast and lay it to one side.

Carving a T-bone or porterhouse steak. Use a small carving knife. Place steak on platter with flank (tail of steak) at carver's left. Cut around the T-bone to free it from the meat. Lay the bone to one side. Cut clear across the steak, making uniform wedge-shaped portions. Cut the flank into serving pieces. In serving, place on each plate a piece of the larger or top muscle, a piece of tenderloin, and, if desired, a piece of the flank.

Carving a rolled rib roast. Use a large carving knife. Place the roast on a platter with the cut surface down. Insert fork, guard up, into the left side of the roast, an inch or two from the top. Make slices across the grain, starting at the far right side. Remove each cord only as you approach it. Cut the cord with the tip of the knife, loosen it with the fork, and lay it to one side.

Carving a blade-bone pot roast. Use a small carving knife. With the point of the knife, cut around the blade bone and remove it. Trim off other bones. If the roast is thin, slice across muscles. For thicker roasts, turn the section on its side and carve across the grain.

Carving a pork loin roast. Have the backbone loosened from the roast at market. When you take the roast out of the oven, remove the backbone before sending the roast to the table. Place the roast on the platter with the rib ends up, and rib side of the roast in front of the carver. Insert fork in the top of the roast. Slice downward between the ribs, to make chop-sized

servings. If the loin roast is a large one, it is possible to
serve a boneless slice between each rib.

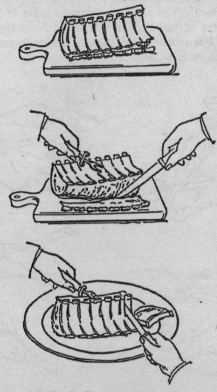

How to carve fowl. Carver places platter so neck of
bird is to his left, and sticks fork astride breastbone.
Leg and thigh bone are separated from nearest side by
cutting at thigh joint 1, pressing leg away from body.
With carving fork still in place, carver next separates
nearest wing in same manner as he did leg, cutting
around wing joint 2 to locate exact dividing point of
joint. Then he severs wing completely. Now breast

meat is ready to be sliced. Start at angle near tip of breastbone. Cut thin slices of white meat, always working toward joint where wing was removed, as shown in illustration 3. Then separate thigh from leg at joint 4; in the case of turkey, cut thin slices from these two pieces 5. For second helpings, turn platter, repeat same process on other side.

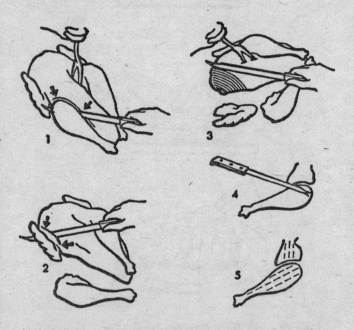

Carving a whole ham. Bring the ham to the table with the "decorated" side up, and the shank to the carver's right. The carver must turn the ham on its side for carving. The leg bone divides the ham into two unequal portions. The thick or chunky side of the ham will yield larger, more attractive slices called "horseshoe" slices. In order to carve these easily, first cut several lengthwise slices off the thinner side to form a base on which to rest the ham during carving.

Now turn the ham on this base and cut a small

wedge-shaped piece from the shank end (where the bone protrudes). This cut should be made just inside the knuckle. Then cut slices right down to bone. When a sufficient number of slices has been cut, slip the knife in at the wedge and cut along the bone to free all of the horseshoe slices at once. For more servings, turn the ham over to its original position and cut slices to the bone.

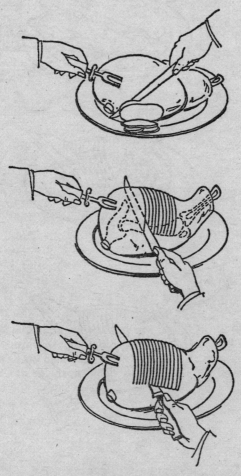

Carving a roast leg of lamb. Bring the lamb to the table on a platter with the shank to the carver's right. Cut two or three slices lengthwise from the near side. This will form a base to make carving easier.

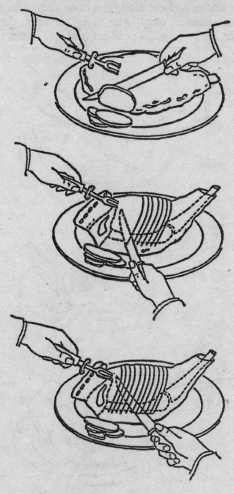

Turn the meat onto the base and, starting at the shank end, cut slices perpendicularly down to the bone, as shown in the illustration.

Free the slices by cutting under them, following the top of the shank bone. Lift the slices out, transferring them to the platter.

4

Fish and Shellfish

THERE'S A WORLD OF DELICIOUS SEAFOOD WAITING TO BE EXPLORED

Seafood can add new taste treats to your menus. You have more varieties than ever to choose from, since modern transportation and refrigeration methods make them available at local markets or fish stores in communities far removed from their native waters.

Most of the water animals used as food in our society belong to two major groups, commonly known as fish and shellfish. The fish, both fresh- and salt-water varieties, are vertebrates—that is, have backbones. They are covered with scales or, occasionally, with just a scaly-looking skin. Shellfish are invertebrates—that is, they lack backbones but are covered with some type of shell.

The shellfish we eat belong to two major subgroups —mollusks and crustaceans. Mollusks, such as clams and oysters, are very soft in their body and are protected by hard shells. The crustaceans, such as lobsters, crabs, shrimps, and crayfish, are covered by segmented, crustlike shells.

In addition to being a delicious food, fish is high in nutritive values. Fish is low in calories (a big plus for weight-conscious gourmets), high in protein, and high in mineral content. This varies from fish to fish, but most fish are mineral-rich, notably in calcium, phosphorus, copper, and iron. Besides this, fish with a relatively high fat content, like salmon or mackerel, contain some vitamins A and D.

BUYING SEAFOOD

Perhaps even more so than with meat, your success in serving tasty seafood depends first upon your buying skill. Fish aren't only seasonal but also regional to some extent. Many varieties are shipped only into the large markets such as New York, Chicago, New Orleans, and San Francisco. In other areas you'll always find the seven favorites—flounder, haddock, mackerel, cod, halibut, ocean perch, and whiting—plus fish from nearby lakes, rivers, bays, or oceans, and a variety of frozen fish and shellfish. As the demand for other varieties increases, they'll become available, so ask for them in your grocery market or at your fish dealer's.

When buying fresh fish, watch for these signs of real freshness:

Eyes—bright, clear, full, transparent, and somewhat protruding. The eyes of stale fish often are cloudy or pink and somewhat sunken.

Skin—shiny and full-colored. Stale fishskin looks faded.

Gills—red and clean-looking. Gills of stale fish are gray, brownish, or greenish.

Flesh—firm and adhering to the bones.

Odor—fresh. "Fishy" odor associated with fish only develops as fish is stored. It should never be disagreeably strong.

Frozen fish have quality standards too:

Odor—Little or no odor. Poor-quality frozen fish has strong fishy odor.

Flesh—solidly frozen with no discoloration or

browning. Fish thawed and refrozen is usually poor in quality.

Wrapping—steaks and fillets should be wrapped in moistureproof material with little or no air space between fish and wrapping.

Glazing—whole fish in the round or dressed are often frozen with a glaze of ice to prevent drying and freezer burn. This should should be intact.

Shellfish—whether being bought live, fresh, or frozen—present special requirements depending on the variety:

Lobsters when bought alive should show movement of the legs and the tail should curl under the body. When cooked in the shell, lobster should be bright red in color and without strong or disagreeable odor. Cooked meat should be white, sweet-smelling, and always held or displayed on ice.

Lobster tails (rock lobster or spiny) are usually sold frozen. They are sections of ocean crayfish. The meat should be whitish, hard-frozen, and odorless.

Crabs should be alive in the shell as hard-shell the year around, or alive in the shell as soft-shell in warm months only. In-the-shell crabs should show movement of the legs if bought alive. When cooked in the shell, they should be bright red in color and without disagreeable odor. Cooked meat should be milky white, sweet-smelling, and always held or displayed on ice.

Crab meat and lobster meat are sold fresh cooked in pry-open cans, useful in quick main dishes as well as in salads.

Shrimp should have firm meat texture, mild odor. Shells are grayish green, pinkish tan, or pink, depending on variety. "Green" shrimp is a market term for shrimps that have not been cooked. Shrimps are usually priced according to size, the larger ones higher in price. Size, however, does not affect quality.

Scallops are sold shucked, fresh or frozen. Fresh sea

scallops are white, larger and less expensive than bay scallops, which are creamy, light tan, or pinkish in color. They should have a sweet, pleasant odor and be practically free of liquid.

Oysters should be alive in the shell, tightly closed. Gaping shells that do not close when tapped indicate dead oysters that should be discarded. Shucked oysters should be creamy in color, plump, with clear liquor, and free from pieces of shell. The liquor should not exceed ten per cent by weight of the total.

Clams should be alive in the shell. If the shell is open, it should close tightly when tapped. Discard any clams that remain open. Shucked clams should be creamy in color, plump, with clear liquor, and free from pieces of shell.

Mussels should be alive in the shells, which should be closed—or at least the shells should be tighter when tapped. Shucked mussels are not sold in fish stores but can be bought in cans.

COOKING TIPS

Fish differs from meat. Though fish is protein food, its water content is higher than that of meat and its extractives are lower. This means that the flavor of fish is delicate. Meat cookery is more concerned with tenderness and the development of flavor. Fish and some shellfish are already tender, so cooking must develop flavor.

Turn thick steaks and whole fish once, when broiling. Follow directions for fillets, broiling 3 to 8 minutes before turning, depending on thickness of fish. Brush with melted butter after turning, sprinkle with seasonings, and broil second side.

Broil fish with imagination. Place tomatoes, mushroom caps, and baked potatoes, split in half and topped with cheese, in broiler pan around your fish. Broil all to a beautiful color picture.

Metal foil boats help eliminate cleaning chores after broiling and baking, help you remove fish unbroken from pan.

Off with its head? Only after baking. If head is cut off before baking fish, the cut end dries and toughens. Leaving the head on during baking seals in the flavor and juices and shortens cooking time.

What causes the fish odor isn't so much the fish itself as the smoking fat. Solution: Be careful to keep the frying fat from reaching the smoking point. (A fat thermometer is surest way to control fat temperature when deep-fat frying.)

The fish that didn't get away. Those fish needn't be so slippery when you handle them if you first dip your fingers in salt.

Lean fish is clean fish (fat fish, too) and requires only a dip in salt cold water and wiping dry. Don't hold fish or seafood under running water.

"Butter up" your fish by using butter generously in cooking and in fish sauces. Butter brings out the best in every one of them.

Rare tidbit in rarebit: Leftover or canned seafood makes a welcome rarebit difference. Add tomato juice instead of milk and see for yourself.

Fish stock plus gelatin equals aspic. This is a jelly made from fish stock. Stock is boiled down enough to become firm when cold, then is thickened with gelatin. Adds festive touch to salads, side dishes, lunches.

In addition to the fish and shellfish described here, there are many other aquatic inhabitants that many peoples, especially in other parts of the world, enjoy eating. Eels, to name one, are highly prized and make tasty fare: all you need do is get over any prejudices about eels' appearance and reputation. Still another variety of seafood popular among many peoples is squid. There are several ways of serving them, but one of the tastiest is to deep-fry them like onion rings. Squid are easily cleaned (and virtually odorless). When clean, the hollow bodies may be sliced in ½ to ¾-inch bands; these are then tossed in a lightly seasoned flour and placed gently in hot cooking oil; fry 15–20 minutes, remove and drain excess fat, and serve with slice of lemon.

STORING SEAFOOD

Keep fresh fish fresh. Fresh fish is tastiest when eaten soon after you bring it home. Flavor decreases in a few days, even when fish stays otherwise fresh. Refrigerate to keep but do not freeze store-purchased fresh fish.

Keep frozen fish frozen. Frozen fish should be stored in the freezing compartment of your refrigerator or in your home freezer until ready to use. Once thawed, don't refreeze frozen fish. Don't thaw completely before preparing, only enough to let outside lose its icy rigidity. Flavor drains away with melting ice.

Shellfish: Treat same as fish. For live shellfish, keep in refrigerator at medium temperature but do not place in water.

When the family fisherman (or fisheress) brings home more fish than you can use conveniently, choose what you want to cook immediately, then freeze the rest.

5

Vegetables

ALL YOU NEED TO KNOW ABOUT BUYING, STORING, PREPARING, AND SERVING

Careful selection of fresh foods makes all the difference in what your table gains and your wallet loses, and nowhere is this truer than with buying vegetables. When you want vegetables just right—fresh, solid, ripe, attractive—pay for the best: when you start throwing away parts of your "bargain" buys, you are probably losing most of the pennies you saved.

But if the vegetables are to be cooked or prepared in some way, if the appearance doesn't count, perhaps you should look around for cheaper varieties. Vegetable stands sometimes set aside "seconds," slightly bruised vegetables or those that have passed their prime. If the price is considerably less, these may be real bargains.

Refrigerator can revive bargain vegetables. Many food dealers will sell slightly wilted leafy vegetables at reduced price. Before storing, wash them; place in crisper drawer while still moist. Process often restores crispness completely.

Don't throw away beet tops. They are delicious and are rich in vitamins and minerals, especially iron.

Many people discard celery tops. Chop and use them in salads, soups, stuffings, sandwich spreads, and stews. They add flavor.

Don't buy squishy squash. Save money on squash. Select only squash that is heavy for its size, with clear complexion and firm, smooth rinds. Blemishes and scars and soft rinds may mean you're wasting your money.

Quality counts. In choosing fruits and vegetables for freezing, buy the best. Properly packaged, you get out of the freezer exactly what you put into it. Freezing does not improve low-grade foods.

STORING VEGETABLES

The storing story. Generally, fresh green vegetables are most safely stored in the refrigerator if not used the same day you bring them home. Still there are a few little tricks to know:

Certain vegetables keep better if stored "as is." Peas and lima beans should be stored in the pod and corn in the husk (to preserve full food value and prevent shriveling).

Keep corn on the cob fresh. When you have to keep it a day or longer before serving, corn on the cob can be kept juicy and fresh in this way: Slice a small piece off the stalk end and stand ears in a pan containing an inch of water. Let the outside leaves stay on.

Goes to their heads. The tops of carrots, beets, turnips, and parsnips should be cut off before the vegetables are stored. The tops draw the moisture and food value from the roots, leaving them wilted and limp.

Keeping parsley fresh. Place in a fruit jar, close lid tight, and keep in the refrigerator.

FREEZING VEGETABLES

To freeze or not to freeze, that is the question. Each vegetable reacts in a different way. It's worth knowing for sure.

Let the government help you. Some varieties of vegetables and fruits are better adapted to freezing than others. When planting a garden or buying vegetables for freezing, consult the Agricultural Extension Service Department at your state university to learn about varieties grown in your locality that are considered best for freezing.

Do not freeze lettuce, celery, raw tomatoes or carrots. They lose crispness when frozen.

To prepare vegetables for freezing, first sort, then clean and wash in cold water. Work with quantities of no more than a pound at a time. After washing, scald or steam. Either method of heating prevents loss of flavor, color, and texture (because it retards action of enzymes).

Get 'em while they're young. With few exceptions (such as winter squash and eggplant), buy "young" vegetables, before their starch content has developed. Prepare for freezing immediately after harvest or purchase. If this is impossible, store in refrigerator, but not for more than eight hours.

Test corn before freezing. Corn loses flavor rapidly after picking and must be prepared for freezing as soon after harvest as possible. Choose only ears of best maturity and variety. Quality can be determined by testing kernels. Kernels should fill the ear and their "milk" should be thin and sweet, nor starchy. Ears chosen for corn on the cob should be even less mature.

Newest wrinkle in freezing corn on the cob. Remove husks from corn and wrap each ear individually in heavyweight freezer aluminum foil. Place wrapped ears in rapidly boiling water and blanch eight minutes. Chill in the refrigerator for an hour. Freeze as usual. To reheat after freezing, place in cold water directly from freezer, then bring to the boiling point. In this way corn thaws while water is heating. (If corn is to be held only one or two months it can be wrapped in lightweight aluminum foil.)

PREPARING VEGETABLES

When washing green vegetables (spinach, kale, broccoli, etc.), add salt to the water and allow to soak for a few minutes. Any foreign matter clinging to them will float to surface.

Laundering spinach. You'll save many, many washings if you soak spinach first in salt water. (P.S. If you like your spinach with a nice, fresh green color, cook it uncovered, in only the water that clings to the leaves after the final rinse.)

Wash leafy vegetables, such as spinach, just before cooking. Add no water; enough clings to the leaves, from washing water, to cook them.

Clean newly dug garden vegetables easily. Place in wire egg-gathering basket and spray with garden hose. Basket holds generous supply of vegetables.

How to "chop" parsley. Away with the tedious old wooden bowl and chopping tool. Separate tufts from stems. Either cut the parsley with one of the new patented cutters or gather it firmly in the left hand, cutting through it with a knife or scissors until it is very fine.

You'll grate carrots without sustaining wounds if you leave at least an inch of the green tops on. Use them as handles and you can grate the vegetable with ease. If you buy the kind of carrot that is packaged without tops, "snack" between meals on the last half-inch bit of raw carrot. It's loaded with vitamin A and has practically no calories. You won't gain an ounce if you eat it.

To extract juice from an onion. Cut a slice and scrape the onion over the finest part of your grater. Or simply scrape a sharp knife across the cut edge, working over a small bowl. You'll soon have that teaspoonful that many recipes call for. Skip the bowl, if you have a sense of adventure, and scrape the juice right into the mixture that calls for onion juice. A few drops more or less don't matter and you save washing one dish.

Know your onions and shed no tears. Next time you slice onions, spear a 1-inch chunk of bread on the point of your paring knife before peeling. Bread absorbs those tear-jerking fumes.

Beets peel easily if they are dipped in cold water immediately after they are boiled. Don't soak 'em, though. They bleed easily. And remember to leave about an inch of stem on beets when you cook them. Cut too close, they really bleed.

For crisp celery, immerse in ice-cold water, with a couple of ice cubes added for good measure, for a few moments before serving.

COOKING TIPS

Preserve vitamins and minerals by cooking vegetables as little as possible. Avoid peeling if you can. If skins must come off, pare thinly. To preserve natural color, leave pot uncovered for first few minutes of cooking.

To cook frozen or fresh vegetables at their best, use smallest practical amount of water. Use saucepan with tight-fitting lid. After cooking and draining (saving cooking liquor for other purposes, such as making soups and gravies), add bit of butter or margarine and keep at warm or simmer heat until serving time.

Food-saver. When food cooked in water has been oversalted, boil a few pieces of raw potato in the pot for several minutes. Most of the excess salt will be absorbed by the potatoes.

Avoid the overflow. A small piece of butter added to the cooking water prevents vegetables, macaroni, or rice from boiling over. Keeping heat low, once boiling has begun, is another trick to control the situation.

Frozen stew. When preparing stew for freezing, do not cook vegetables completely. They will finish cooking when the stew is thawed and reheated. Omit potatoes from frozen stew and add them, fresh-cooked, when stew is ready to use.

Rice trick. Keep rice grains snowy-white and separate, instead of lumpy, by adding a teaspoonful of lemon juice to the water.

Another trick with rice. Place washed rice in a casserole dish, add a can of consommé, cover, and bake at 350° F. for an hour. Rice comes out fluffy without watching. Consommé adds flavor.

Whiter cauliflower. Cauliflower will come to the table much whiter if a piece of lemon is added during cooking. And cook only until tender. Overcooking also tends to darken cauliflower.

IDEAS FOR
LEFTOVER VEGETABLES

Leftover vegetables can give you a delicious treat. Place them in layers in a casserole, add cream sauce, sprinkle with grated cheese, and bake.

Peas pep up leftovers. If vegetables such as string beans, broccoli, corn, carrots, or beets are among your leftovers, use them with canned peas in a mixed-vegetable salad served with French or Russian dressing.

Add a few empty pea pods to peas and to soup when cooking; they add flavor. But fish them out before serving either; they're too tough to eat except when they are garden-fresh and cooked with tender young peas, when you eat pod and all.

Cauliflower stalks are usually thrown away from force of habit. They are delicious cooked and served with a cheese or Hollandaise sauce.

A few leftover **string beans** can be added to chopped celery and finely chopped onion for a nutritious and delicious sandwich filling. Moisten the mixture with mayonnaise or other salad dressing.

A little leftover **spinach,** finely chopped, adds intrigue and color to the batter for luncheon waffles. Or, mixed with chopped hard-cooked eggs in a white sauce, it becomes part of a topping for waffles.

Save leftover **broccoli** to decorate next day's casserole of whipped potatoes. Push stems into potatoes, with just the blossoms showing. Brush with melted butter or margarine and put in oven at 350° F., to brown, for about 15 minutes.

Quick oats have many uses as leftovers. Brown some in butter or margarine for "crumbs" to top a vegetable or other casserole dish. Or use the oats instead of part of all the nuts called for in your favorite brownie recipe. Brown and crisp in butter or margarine before using oats as nuts, both on brownies and for topping.

Old friends, new faces. For treat flavor, try dipping tomatoes, eggplant, and such in leftover waffle batter, then sauté lightly. Puts new faces on old favorites and helps the budget no end.

HANDY HINTS FOR WORKING WITH VEGETABLES

Chop, chop—once a week. Why not do the whole week's chopping at one time? Store chopped parsley, peppers, onions, celery, nuts in refrigerator, each in an individually labeled jar.

Corn off the cob. The kernels of sweet corn are a cinch to remove if you use a shoehorn. The wide end of the horn is just right for shearing the kernels off.

An asparagus tip. Always open cans of whole asparagus spears from the bottom so that the tips will not break as you ease the spears out of the can.

Keep the vinegar from sweet pickles (or any other

pickles, for that matter). Serve it in a glass jar for pepping up salads and dressings. Awfully good, for instance, when mixed with potato salad.

Note to K.P.s. Don't throw away half of that highly nutritious potato by peeling it. Rub the skin off, instead, with one of those new metal pot cleaners. These are just rough enough to rub off the outer skin without wasting the body of the potato.

Let them catch their breath. Freshly opened canned vegetables, if allowed to stand for 15 minutes before heating, will regain oxygen they have lost by canning. Makes an amazing difference in flavor.

Popcorn à la hurry. Use your pressure cooker without indicator weight for popping corn. Heat small amount of vegetable oil; add enough corn to almost cover bottom of cooker. Shaking isn't necessary. It should take about five minutes to pop a goodly batch this way.

Fingers stained? Remove vegetable stains from your fingers by rubbing them with a slice of raw potato.

Candid advice on candied vegetables. You love 'em. But you hate washing the pan afterward. Who doesn't? Even an electric dishwasher rebels. Heat the greased pan before adding the sugary mixture. Doesn't it wash a whole lot easier?

Don't waste olives. Next time you serve them, pour a little salad oil over the remainder in the jar. Prevents molding, makes them keep a long time in the refrigerator.

Make your own "olive" oil. Soak four large olives (unstuffed) in cup of salad oil, keeping in tightly covered jar, in the refrigerator for a week.

Refrigerate all vegetable oils, including real olive oil. They become rancid in time, especially in warm summer months, if not refrigerated. If you object to the cloudiness that develops if oil is a little too chilled, simply remove the container from the refrigerator an hour before you plan to use the oil and it will be crystal-clear again.

Pliers ply their trade when you open a jar of home-canned vegetables or fruit. Use the pliers to grip the rubber ring and screw cap loosens in a jiffy.

Kitchen shears share kitchen chores. They beat a knife for removing seeds and pulp from peppers you're preparing for stuffing. To save their flavor, cut chives and tarragon with shears, instead of chopping. Use shears in cutting parsley, for dicing cooked meats, giblets, for cutting crusts from bread, and to cut marshmallows and raisins. (Dip shears in flour before cutting sticky substances.)

Identify with glamour. Save those good-enough-to-eat pictures of fruits and vegetables from the magazines, then paste them on the appropriate jars when you do your canning. Makes each one look more appetizing.

6

Dairy Products and Eggs

BASIC TO THE DIET, DELICIOUS TO THE TASTE, BUT PERISHABLE IF NOT HANDLED PROPERLY

Milk stays fresh longer if not allowed to stand at room temperature for any length of time, so don't remove until actually needed. Return unused milk to refrigerator promptly.

Fresh milk stays fresh longer if you add a pinch of salt to a quart of fresh milk.

Store milk in the coldest part of your refrigerator, at about 40° F., to protect its flavor and food value. If it cannot be kept cold, use milk as soon as possible. To save the riboflavin, one of milk's important vitamins, keep container away from strong light.

A partially emptied milk container should be re-covered with the closure provided. Uncovered milk quickly picks up flavors of other nearby foods.

If you use milk for coffee or tea, empty the cream pitcher back into the covered refrigerator container; don't store it in the uncovered pitcher.

Before boiling milk, rinse the pan in cold water. Keeps milk from sticking to the pan. But it doesn't keep it from boiling over, so keep an eye on it and turn off heat the minute milk boils.

Milk may be heated, for yeast-dough making, custards, and other mixtures, in the top of a double boiler set over boiling water. That way you don't have to worry about boiling over or possibly scorching milk over direct heat.

After opening can of evaporated milk, plug the openings with neat little rolls of waxed paper. Keeps can holes from being sealed over with dried milk, lets milk pour freely when plugs are removed. Also, contents are less likely to spill if the can is accidentally tipped—and the milk won't take on odors from other foods in the refrigerator.

Cream won't curdle. We've all been annoyed at the way cream tends to curdle when poured over acid berries or fruits, spoiling the appearance though the taste's the same. Avoid this by mixing a tiny pinch of baking soda with the cream before serving.

Cream whips faster. To whip cream in record time, add 6 or 8 drops of lemon juice per pint (2 cups) of cream. Use an eye dropper and count them; too much lemon sours the cream.

CHEESE

Cheese can replace milk. For children (up to 80) who do not like milk, cheese can be used to add flavor and milk values to meals. For instance, 1¼ ounces of yellow cheese equals many of the food values contained in a whole cup of milk. They share many fine nutritive qualities, of course, since cheese is made from milk.

Store perishable soft cheese, as you do milk, in the refrigerator in a tightly covered container. Buy in amounts to be used in a short time. Other cheeses keep well in a cold place if wrapped so that air is kept out. Foil is fine for this.

Refrigerate packaged cheese in its original container, using additional waxed paper or aluminum foil, if necessary, to rewrap the cheese. Wrap unpackaged cheese tightly with waxed paper, laminated foil, a vinegar-dampened cloth, or similar wrapping before refrigerating. An overwrap that's convenient for paper or cloth is non-porous pliofilm bag such as you use in freezer storage.

If mold forms on cheese, it may be scraped away with no harm to the cheese. Should cheese become dry, grate it and keep in covered container. It's good for cooking even if no longer attractive in solid form.

Cheese (except cottage) tastes best when served unchilled. Take it from the refrigerator long enough before serving to reach room temperature.

To prevent curdling, scorching, and stringiness in foods made with cheese or milk, cook at low, low temperatures and don't overcook.

Easy-to-cut cheese. Warm the knife and it's no trick at all to slice cheese as easily as butter. But there are cheese cutters, too, that are just as easy to use.

Cheese grates easily if it has been chilled first. So grate it the moment you take it from the refrigerator.

BUTTER

Butter keeps better if you keep it clean, cold, covered, to protect its delicate flavor and texture. Leave it in original protective wrapping until ready to use. Some refrigerators have temperature-controlled butter compartments to keep butter spreadable. Keep only two or three days' supply in such compartments, even though they're sized to fit a pound block of butter.

Easy-to-spread consistency is best achieved by setting on a small plate or butter dish the amount of butter you will require to spread on bread and leaving this at room temperature for about 10 minutes. Melting or quick melting of unnecessarily large quantities spoils freshness of the butter you don't use right away.

EGGS

Tips on egg storage. Always keep in refrigerator. Unbroken eggs should be in covered containers; otherwise they lose moisture and absorb odors, because shells are porous. Yolks keep best if covered with water; whites should be kept in a tightly covered jar.

To keep eggs fresh for a fairly long time, rub very fresh eggs with oil, butter, or pure glycerin over the entire surface of the shell.

If you keep all your eggs in one basket, pencil-mark leftover eggs, so that you'll use them up first.

To test the age of an egg, place in deep pan of cold water. If it lies on its side, it is fresh. If it stands at an angle, it is probably 3 or 4 days old. If the egg stands on end upright, it is over 10 days old. If it floats to the top, toss it out!

Is that stray egg hard-cooked or raw? To test, place the egg on its side and spin it like a top. If the egg spins on an even keel, it is cooked. If it wobbles, it's raw.

Don't freeze cooked foods containing hard-cooked egg whites. Egg white changes in texture rapidly, toughens, and tends to develop off flavors when frozen.

Grade B eggs make grade A meals. While you need Grade A eggs for boiling or poaching, the cheaper Grade Bs are fine for scrambling and general cooking purposes. For additional savings in baking, use dried eggs.

The least understood and most important rule in egg cookery is—low temperature. The science behind the rule is that the protein in the egg is easily toughened by too-high temperature. This accounts for eggs of unappetizing texture that give away the third-rate cook.

Cold-water start is recommended for simmering eggs if eggs are taken right from the refrigerator, because sudden temperature changes tend to crack shells. If you are in a hurry, though, try running hot water over the eggs and immediately draining it off. That scares them a little but not to the cracking point. Then add more hot water and cook.

"Seal" broken eggshell immediately if it cracks during cooking. How? Just add a little vinegar to the cooking water.

Egg-peeling tip. By adding salt to the water in which eggs are hard-cooked, you harden the shell and make it much easier to peel off. A quick dunk in cold water helps too, as does rolling the egg around to crush the shell somewhat before you begin peeling.

To prevent egg white from spreading when poached, add 1 teaspoon salt or a few drops of vinegar to each cup of water used for poaching. Helps to hasten coagulation of egg white. A little swirl of the water around the egg with a spoon helps too.

To separate egg whites and yolks, the for-sure no-broken-yolk way, puncture a small hole at one end of the shell. This releases the white into a collecting bowl and yolk stays inside. Break shell, remove yolk whole.

It's best to open eggs in separate bowl before adding to mixed batter. Avoids spoiling entire mixture should one egg prove bad. Keeps shells out of batter too.

Best way to divide an egg. After beating the egg, measure it in a measuring cup, pour off half, save the rest for scrambled eggs. Cover the leftover beaten egg, stored in a custard cup, with aluminum foil.

When beating egg whites, be sure to use an enamel, stainless-steel, glass, or porcelain bowl. Never use aluminum, because eggs darken aluminumware.

Egg whites beat up quicker and higher if you add a tiny pinch of salt and let them stand until they're room temperature before you beat them.

How many eggs? Most recipes call for average-sized eggs (medium to large). If using small eggs, allow about 3½ tablespoons slightly mixed whole egg for each egg in the recipe.

7

Soups

HOMEMADE, CANNED, OR FROZEN—HERE ARE TIPS ON HOW TO MAKE THE MOST OUT OF SOUPS

Whatever you boil, whether meat, poultry, fish, vegetables, all yield wonderful stock for a soup base. Even if all you do about soup is to open a can of ready-to-dilute condensation, add liquids saved from cooking. They give you a bonus of extra-fresh flavor and vitamins.

Any French cook will tell you it is an unforgivable waste to throw away those outside lettuce leaves, even when they are wilted. They make a wondrously tasty extra for homemade soup.

Old spice, new tang. Have you tried a few cloves in your vegetable soup? Even to this classic soup they give an exciting new lift in flavor.

To remove fat from soup (and from yourself), dip an ice cube wrapped in piece of clean cloth into soup. Fat congeals quickly on a cold surface.

OFF-BEAT WAYS WITH SOUP

On a diet? Try soup on the rocks. Simply pour good beef bouillon, your own or right from a can, over ice cubes in a tall glass. Swish around to chill, then drink. You'll find it light and refreshing. Plain, or with a twist of lemon peel, soup on the rocks has become a national favorite beverage.

Don't like eggs? Everyone should eat an occasional egg, at least three a week. For those who don't care for eggs a soupnog may be the answer. Use a rotary beater to blend 1 can cream of chicken, celery, or mushroom soup with 1 can milk. Chill. Just before serving, beat in an egg for each portion. Serve ice cold. Good with tomato soup too.

Purée is pure delight. A delicious soup, made with food put through a ricer and thinned with cream or stock. Example: split-pea soup. Don't let it stick to the pot and burn. Stir frequently while the soup cooks. And try cooking it in an aluminum pot. Try making puréed soups, too, by using a blender. You can begin with raw foods and liquids if you have a blender and use it to make soup.

Vary your cold-soup story. Stock your refrigerator with cans of consommé, to serve jellied with diced avocado and lemon wedges; bouillon to serve full-strength on the rocks, over ice cubes; cream of chicken to which you add cold milk.

A chilled-soup special. Combine cream of mushroom soup with cream of chicken, 1 can of each. Stir in 1 can of water and 1 can of milk. Add ½ cup chopped shrimp (canned or fresh-cooked), then chill thoroughly before serving. Chill serving dishes too.

QUICK AND EASY MEALS
WITH SOUP

Save time and please the family by cooking with soup. Here are six one-dish meals that have a soup base:

1. Combine undiluted cream of celery soup with ½ cup milk and 1 cup or more of grated sharp cheese.

Heat slowly until cheese melts, stirring frequently. Add 4 cups cooked macaroni, spaghetti, or noodles, and a little chopped, sautéed green pepper and onion. Heat and serve.

2. *In a skillet or saucepan* combine 1 can cream of mushroom soup, ½ cup evaporated milk, a 7-ounce can drained flaked tuna, 1 cup cooked peas or other vegetable, and 1 cup crushed potato chips. Heat and serve with a generous sprinkling of chopped parsley on top.

3. *Sauté 1 chopped onion* and a slivered green pepper in a tablespoon of hot fat. Stir in 1 can undiluted chicken gumbo soup and several tablespoons chili sauce. Taste and season. Add 2 cups cooked shrimp. Cook until thickened. Serve over plenty of hot cooked rice.

4. *Combine soup with leftovers.* Add a can of Scotch broth, undiluted, to leftover diced or chopped cooked meat, vegetables, and gravy. Add a bit of chopped onion for tang, some chopped black olives for glamour. Turn into a casserole or other baking dish and top with mashed potatoes, biscuits, or pastry, and bake, at 400° F., until topping is baked or browned and casserole piping hot.

5. *Another casserole idea* to please the family. Sauté several strips bacon until crisp. Remove from pan. Brown chopped onion in the bacon drippings. Stir in 1 can undiluted tomato soup, 4 cups cooked drained lima beans, and the bacon, broken up. Turn into a casserole, spread with buttered bread crumbs, and bake until brown.

6. *An egg stretcher uses soup.* Heat 1 can cream of mushroom soup with ¼ cup milk. Gently stir in 4 or 5 sliced or quartered hard-cooked eggs and some chopped stuffed olives. Heat. Serve on hot buttered toast, toasted English muffins, or hot split biscuits.

SOUP TOPPINGS AND
ACCOMPANIMENTS

To top it all. Any canned or homemade soup may be given a company touch by topping the servings with a mixture of beaten egg white, plenty of real mayonnaise, and a dash of salt. Add a spoonful to the top of each serving of soup and garnish with finely chopped parsley.

Different bread sticks to serve with soup may be quickly made from stale bread. Trim crusts and spread both sides of bread with real mayonnaise. Toast in waffle iron until brown. Cut each slice into three fingers.

Heat thin slices of frankfurters in lentil or pea soup for ten minutes. They'll float on top when you serve the soup. They go well with bean soup too.

Two ways with croutons. Cut stale bread into small cubes. Sauté in butter until golden brown, stirring frequently for uniform color. A quick way to make croutons in quantity is to fry them in hot, deep fat. If you have a fat thermometer, heat fat to 375° F. If you haven't, a test crouton should be brown in 1 minute.

Hot popcorn doesn't have to be fresh-popped as a soup topper. Heat plain or cheese-flavored popcorn in a 350° F. oven, in a brown paper bag, for 5 to 10 minutes. It's a good topper for cream of spinach soup or other bland cream soups.

Whipped cream, lightly salted and sprinkled with paprika, is a quick-and-easy but elegant soup topper.

Sautéed Taylor ham cubes make a hearty topping for rich pea soup, lentil or bean soup. Cut the ham crouton-size and sauté in butter or margarine or in any bacon drippings you may have on hand.

Old-fashioned cracklings for New England fish chowder. Cut ¼ pound salt pork in small pieces and sauté in a large kettle or Dutch oven. Cook and stir until the fat has been extracted. Remove cracklings and drain on paper toweling. Use the fat as the base for making fish chowder. Serve chowder with cracklings sprinkled on top.

Custard garnish. Beat together 3 egg yolks, 2 tablespoons milk, dash of cayenne, and a little salt. Pour into small pie plate or other small oven pan, so that there is a ¼ to ½ inch layer of custard. Set plate in a pan of hot water and bake at 350° F. for 20 minutes, or until set. Cool and dice. Makes a wonderful garnish for a clear consommé.

8

Breads, Rolls, and Biscuits

THE STAFF OF LIFE CAN ALSO BE THE LIFE OF THE PARTY

Tips that keep bread fresh. If you store bread in a room-temperature place, such as your breadbox, it will stay soft but may not keep too long, especially in warm weather. If you store it in your refrigerator it will be safe from mold but will not remain soft. Compromise is to store bread in the refrigerator but wrap it first in waxed paper or other moisture-proof paper and then tuck it into a pliofilm bag. Double wrapping keeps moisture in, refrigerator temperature keeps molds out.

If you use lots of bread, store it in your breadbox. But be sure to keep the box clean and free of old pieces of bread. Scald and/or sun it weekly.

If you use little bread but have a freezing compartment in your refrigerator, double-wrap the bread as directed for refrigerator storage and store bread in the frozen-food compartment. You can keep several kinds of bread frozen simultaneously, have a choice of breads, and use only as much as you need for one meal.

Can you freeze bakery bargains? Baked foods (including yeast rolls, yeast bread, quick breads, cookies, unfrosted cakes and some frosted ones, and cupcakes) can be frozen for from two to three months. Buy them when your baker features specials, eat them when you want them. (See pages 91–96 for more details on frozen foods and home freezers.)

Know your bread flours. Flour milled from hard wheat is best for bread baking. (Leave the soft wheat type of flour for fine-textured cakes.) For quick breads, biscuits, muffins (and some pastries), the "all-purpose" flours are well suited.

Whole-grain flours for highest food value. Whole-wheat, graham, and rye flours have exceptionally high nutritional content. They're a better buy, nutritionally, than white flour, better even than "enriched" white flour. Soya flour, generally used in combination with wheat flours for home baking, adds valuable protein content. Use ratio of one part soya flour to nine parts wheat flour.

To prevent bread crust from cracking, shelter fresh-baked bread from cold gusts of air or sudden drafts and winds on the heated surface.

It does matter how you slice it. If sliced too soon after it has been removed from the oven, fresh bread tends to compress and collapse. Be patient—and gentle. Then use a serrated bread knife, and you should be able to slice the bread as smoothly as if it were done by a machine.

To freshen French bread, Italian bread, hard rolls, cover crusts with cold water, using a pastry brush. Then place in 350° F., oven until crisp again, about 10 minutes. Cool before slicing.

Roll your dried bread crumbs or cereal crumbs the easy way. Place them between folds of a clean towel or sheets of waxed paper, then roll them. Let no crumbs scatter when grinding dried bread. Catch them in a paper bag. Fasten opening of bag firmly around grinder outlet with tightly tied cord or a rubber band.

Salt cartons into bread-crumb boxes. Empty salt cartons with spouts make excellent containers for bread crumbs ground from dried bread. Use funnel to get crumbs into carton.

ROLLS

To heat ready-to-eat bread and rolls, wrap bread slices or rolls snugly in aluminum foil. Bake at 350° F. about 15 minutes, or until hot. If served in the foil wrapping, turn foil edges down to form a basket; they'll keep hot to the last crumb.

Add your own trimmings to hot-roll mixes. Make hot-cross buns from hot-roll mix by adding raisins to the dough as well as chopped citron, granulated sugar, cinnamon. Then let rise as directed on package, until double in bulk. Shape ball-like buns. Place in greased cake pan. Let rise in warm place for another 30 to 60 minutes. With scissors, cut small cross in each bun. Bake at 400° F. 15 to 20 minutes, or until done. Combine confectioners' sugar with a little warm milk and vanilla extract to dip over hot bun and fill crosses.

Brown 'n' serve rolls come raised and almost completely baked. You bake them another few minutes, following package directions, to bring out the golden color in the crust. You may bake them with your special sweet-mixture topping made with honey, nuts, caramel, orange, brown sugar, or cooked prunes.

BISCUIT WIZARDRY

For light, flaky biscuits, this is the way to handle ingredients: As milk is added to dry ingredients, work latter lightly away from the bottom of mixing bowl with a fork. Then press the bits of dough into a ball. Do not knead. Pat out dough on floured board and roll lightly, outward from center. Never roll back and forth.

Biscuits bake best on baking sheet without sides. To insure proper heat circulation, sheets should be small enough to leave one or two inches of space between edges of sheet and sides and back of oven.

No more pale-face biscuits. Wan-looking baking-powder biscuits turn a healthy golden brown if you simply add a teaspoonful of sugar to the dry ingredients.

Start with a biscuit mix and use your imagination. You can make quick and succulent breakfast hot bread this way: Roll a recipe of biscuit mix into rectangular shape, about ¼ inch thick. Spread with melted butter or margarine. Sprinkle with brown sugar, raisins, and chopped nuts. Roll as you would a jelly roll. Cut into ½-inch slices. Bake on a greased cookie sheet, cut side up, at 425° F. for 15 to 18 minutes.

Leftover biscuit pinwheels. You can use up leftover cooked meat, chicken, or fish and make good use of leftover gravies by using prepared biscuit mix. Roll out a recipe ¼-inch thick, in oblong shape. Grind up leftover meat or other protein with a small raw onion. Add a little tomato catsup, seasonings, and a little leftover gravy. Mix well. Then spread on biscuit dough. Roll as for jelly roll. Cut in ½-inch slices. Bake on greased baking sheet, cut side up, at 425° F. for 15 to 18 minutes. Serve with leftover gravy, mushroom or tomato sauce.

The biscuit mix need not make biscuits. Waffles, pancakes, dumplings, nut bread, fudge cake, chocolate-chip cookies, and breakfast crumb cake are only a few of the goodies you can make with biscuit mix. Simply follow package directions at first, then let yourself go on other uses for biscuit mix.

Bake 'n' eat biscuits come mixed, rolled, and cut, ready for the oven. If you keep a package on hand, store it in the refrigerator, never on the pantry shelf or in your home freezer. It needs refrigerator cold and no more. Before baking, you may add your own sharp or sweet topping, or sprinkle butter-brushed top with poppy seed, caraway or celery seed. Bake at 425° F. for 10 to 15 minutes, or as package directs.

Kitchenette pizza before you say good night. Place three bake 'n' eat biscuits on cookie sheet, with sides touching, cloverleaf fashion. Place ½-inch cube of cheese on each. Top each cube with teaspoonful of chili sauce. Sprinkle with grated Parmesan, garlic salt, dried thyme, salt, pepper. Drizzle on a little salad oil. Bake at 550° F. 5 to 8 minutes.

Coffee-ettes after you say good morning. First dip bake 'n' eat biscuits into melted butter, then into mixture of granulated sugar, cinnamon, chopped nuts. Bake in greased pan or cookie sheet at 425° F. for 20 to 25 minutes.

LET YOURSELF GO WITH BAKING SHORT CUTS

Mixes mix in good company. Even though you're pressed for time, you can still have home-baked hot biscuits, muffins, and other breads if you begin with a mix. All you do is follow package directions and bake. Make hot rolls and buns with mixes too. Just mix and bake as package directs.

Super bread sticks can be made from frankfurter rolls by quartering them lengthwise. Spread cut slices, on all sides, with soft butter or salad oil. Roll in minced parsley, chives, or grated Parmesan cheese. Bake at 425° F. for 5 to 10 minutes.

Don't halve English muffins with a knife. To split, insert fork into side of English muffin until fork reaches center, then repeat all around. Spread torn surfaces with butter or margarine. Toast in toaster or broiler. Or spread first with cream cheese topped with jelly or grated Cheddar cheese, crumbled blue cheese, or cinnamon mixed with sugar and topped with chopped nuts, or nippy soft cheese topped with sliced olives. Then toast in broiler.

Corn muffinettes. Split corn muffins. Top with drizzle of molasses, add chopped nuts, and broil.

Petite toast, as new for breakfast as the morning headlines. Slice hard rolls or French bread into rings ½ to ¾ inch thick. Dip into your favorite French-toast mixture and sauté as usual. This is particularly good with whole-wheat rolls.

Toast for taste. Cut loaf of unsliced raisin bread into squares. Brush cut square surfaces, as well as top and bottom, with melted butter. Sprinkle with sugar and cinnamon. Bake at 375° F. for about 15 minutes, or until golden.

9

Cakes and Pies

BASICS AND SHORTCUTS FOR FINE CAKES AND PLEASING PIES

Mixes are time- and money-savers. Follow package directions and you'll bake a perfect cake every time you use a mix. You can even buy them complete to foil pan, made to fit the recipe for a modest-size cake that serves four nicely, and with another container that has frosting ingredients in it.

Take your pick of mixes. You have a choice of white, gold, chocolate, spice, and various other mixes.

When you're a good mixer, have become familiar with a particular cake mix, you may want to vary it slightly by adding ¼ to 1 teaspoon of additional flavoring. And as long as you chop nuts fairly fine and cut up any fruits you may elect to put in the batter, the resulting cake becomes your special creation.

So you mix your own cake? Start with a sound recipe from a reliable tested source. Follow it exactly, without making changes or substitutions, unless you have made a particular recipe often enough to risk experimenting. Even then, only change flavoring or add solids such as chopped nuts and fruits. Why bother to change a recipe you know is good when you can simply select another from the many thousands published?

You need a baking routine. Read recipe carefully, start only when you really understand it. Determine how you will combine ingredients, assemble ingredients, assemble utensils, prepare pans for baking, making sure they're the proper size and kind.

Do first things first. Chop nuts, heat oven to specified temperature, sift the flour just before measuring it, separate eggs, etc.

Have standard measuring equipment and use it scrupulously, accurately. Never guess. Measure.

Important measuring tools. Two measuring cups (one for dry ingredients, the other for liquids) and one or two sets of measuring spoons are basic when you bake.

Ways to measure shortening. Press into measuring cup or tablespoon and pack lightly, scraping top flat with a spatula or straight knife. Another method is by water displacement. To measure ½ cup shortening, for example, first half fill cup with water. Add shortening by spoonful until water rises to the top of cup. Then drain off water.

In measuring butter, allow ½ pound for 1 cup.

Melted butter or shortening is measured like any liquid.

PANS ARE IMPORTANT

Let the pan fit the cake. For best results, cake batter should only half fill the pan. If you haven't the size pan a recipe calls for, however, select one of the same depth and approximately the same area (length times width).

Warped baking pans cause uneven baking. Warping may cause batter to run to one side of pan and spoil not only appearance but also the quality of the finished product.

Metal pans of light materials are generally best for cakes. They heat quickly, yet reflect heat so that cakes brown delicately.

If cake pan is too shallow, you can build up the sides by lining with a "collar" or strip of heavy brown paper, to give desired height. Paper should be smoothed against greased sides of pan, then the paper itself well greased.

For attractive layer cakes: Insure uniform layers by using straight-sided pans and, if you're a true perfectionist, weighing batter, spooning it into each pan until weights are equal. A household scale works with you on this tip.

Baking insurance. Temper new metal pans before using. Grease them lightly, place in 300° F. oven for an hour or two. Insures better baking results.

If baking recipe calls for greased pan, use very soft or melted shortening. (Butter may be preferred, for flavor.) Dip pastry brush or small piece of crumpled paper toweling in shortening, rub over inside of pan to cover bottom and corners with thin grease film. Greasing sides of baking pans isn't necessary, wastes money and spoils cake's appearance.

Special note for angel-food and sponge cakes. Never grease the pan. These batters need to cling to sides of pan to reach full height. Batter, made up largely of beaten egg whites, is too delicate to hold up and give cake its full volume without support of sides of ungreased pan, to which cake clings during baking and cooling (in inverted pan). Greasing would cause such cakes to fall out of inverted pan while cooling, thus making them flat and soggy.

If you want to bake special-shaped cakes for festive occasions, yet haven't the space to store a lot of special-occasion cake pans, try shaping cake "pans" out of aluminum foil. Using heavy foil double, you can mold it into a heart for an engagement party, a Christmas tree for the Yule season, a star for the Fourth of July, and so on.

Bake 'em oblong, shape 'em later. Another way to have fancy cake shapes is to bake sheet cakes, cut paper patterns in the desired shape, lay the pattern on the cake, and carefully cut cake, using a hot knife, by following the edge of the pattern as you cut. Use left-over pieces of cake for petits fours and in cake-base desserts where the shape's unimportant.

Liners for cake pans. For a good fit, place your pan on several thicknesses of large pieces of waxed paper. Trace around pan with sharp knife. Cut out circle, or the shape pan you've traced. Place one sheet of paper in bottom of pan for one baking. It will be a luxury to have several spare liners handy for future bakings.

IN THE OVEN

Prepare the oven for baking. Be sure oven racks are correctly placed before heating oven. Place racks where heat is most even, so baked product will rise evenly and brown perfectly. Start heating oven early enough before baking so you have even heat of the right temperature before placing in oven to bake. If your oven isn't automatically heat-controlled, keep a reliable oven therometer handy.

Don't crowd your oven. Never try to bake too much at once or place pans too close to oven wall. Heat must circulate freely on all sides of baking pan to give evenly baked results. When using two racks at the same time, do not place one pan directly over the other but stagger them on each rack.

"Baking-is-finished" signals. Usually the time in recipes is exactly right if your oven heat is correct. But, as safeguards, make these tests:

1. Product should have risen to full height and have delicately browned crust.

2. Insert wire cake tester or toothpick near center. It should come out clean and dry.

3. Cake (except sponge cake) should have shrunk away slightly from sides of pan.

4. Press top surface gently with finger. Surface springs back and leaves no imprint if cake is done.

Exceptions: Very rich cakes or chocolate cakes. On these, use only test 1 or 3, because such cakes sometimes cling to tester or may dent slightly when pressed, even though they are thoroughly baked.

THINGS THAT MAKE OR BREAK A CAKE

Cake won't break if you don't try to remove it from the pan before it is sufficiently cooled or cut it while still hot. Otherwise it may crumble.

Cake won't stick. Before placing that delicious cake masterpiece of yours on the plate, spray some powdered sugar over the plate. Keeps the cake from sticking and renders it as maneuverable as it should be.

"Life preserver" for sinking fruits and nuts. If you heat them in the oven, then dust with flour, before adding to cake batter, fruits and nuts won't go to the bottom of the pan.

Your cakes will be light and fluffy if you avoid overstirring or beating batter. Unless cake is very rich, stir after each addition of ingredients only until well blended and smooth. Another precaution: guard against use of too much sugar or liquid, or too little leavening.

Your cake's appearance will be enhanced if you take this simple precaution when putting batter into baking pan: spread batter evenly and away into the corners.

Coarse grain spoils appearance of angel or sponge cake, is usually caused by underbeating egg whites or improper folding when added to the batter. Large holes come from air folded into batter as it is poured into pan. After batter is poured, cut through it with spatula to break large air bubbles and thus eliminate holes.

TIME-SAVERS AND STORAGE HINTS

Electric mixer saves time, energy, does variety of jobs for you. It not only mixes perfect cake batters but also provides short cuts to dozens of interesting desserts, frostings, beverages, and soufflés, chops fruits better than you can by hand.

To maintain freshness, cover any kind of cake, either with a special cover designed to go over a cake pan or with waxed paper. Large cakes may be halved and wrapped for home freezer storage or in the freezing compartment of your refrigerator.

Melt chocolate the easy way. Grease the pan in which you melt chocolate; makes dishwashing easy afterward. Or melt chocolate in little cup made out of two thicknesses of aluminum foil.

Cakes take to freezing. You may bake your cake ahead of time for parties or box lunches, or for unexpected guests.

Frost cake before freezing, if you wish, but remember not all frostings freeze well. If saving time is your motive and you must frost before freezing, don't use seven-minute or egg-type frostings; they become rubbery when frozen.

Frozen cakes will thaw rapidly at room temperature. For best eating quality, they should be served the day you thaw them.

Always refrigerate whipped-cream-frosted cakes, cream-filled cakes, or puff pastries.

Leave fruitcake in original wrapper until ready to serve. Briefly stored, fruitcake may be wrapped in a lint-free cloth. Sprinkle a few drops of brandy or cider over the cloth occasionally to keep cake moist and fresh. For long storage, keep cake in covered metal container that is not entirely airtight.

Serve stale cake fresh, with orange slices, for a quick, attractive hot dessert. Slice cake and top each slice with two slices of orange. Arrange in shallow pan. Cream together a little butter and sugar, stir in an egg yolk and grated orange rind, and spoon over cake and orange slices. Run under broiler five minutes, or until delicately browned.

To freshen stale cake, wrap it in a towel, then put it into a slightly warm oven for a few minutes before serving.

For a novelty dessert treat, try new flavor combinations in your next cake. Delicious blends result from combining two flavors, such as lemon with vanilla, or rose with almond extract.

Use spices sparingly in baking. Measure amounts accurately, because too much spice disguises delicate flavor of baked goods. Sift spices with flour to blend well with other ingredients.

Choose the proper cake plate. Plate should "frame" the cake, be as flat as possible, and extend about two inches beyond edge of cake all the way around. If too large or deep, plate will dwarf the cake. If too small, cake will look giant-clumsy.

THE FINE POINTS IN PIE BAKING

Reason for tough pastry may be in mixing it too long, or handling it too heavily, or using too much water, or not enough shortening. Good pastry is the result of speed, a light hand, and not much rolling.

Extra pie-crust mix a must. Keep one on your shelf as emergency measure. The late hour when you'll be grateful to have it may come early.

Avoid warped pie shells by remembering to add enough prebaking fork pricks and to inspect the pie after five minutes of baking to see if any blisters have appeared that have to be pricked while baking.

Slouching pie shells are a sign of one of two omissions: flutes may not have been pressed to plate firmly enough, or pie has not been chilled for a half hour before baking.

Good pastry greases itself, does not rely on a greased pie plate.

Safe transfer of bottom crust. To eliminate the annoyance of having a fragile round of pie crust break as you are lifting it into the pie plate, roll your crust out on a piece of aluminum foil cut to a circle about 2 inches wider than the pan. With the foil as a guide, you'll find it easy to roll the crust to the right size and shape. Then lift the foil, with the crust on it, and place both in the pie pan with no danger of the crust tearing. You can trim the crust with scissors to the proper size, but leave a fringe of aluminum foil an inch or two wide to catch any juices that may leak from pie and try to run over. And, best of all, the pie plate won't need washing.

To line casseroles and baking dishes with aluminum foil, mold foil over back of utensil, then fit inside. Smooth out and arrange decorative ruffle around top edge of utensil.

Glass bakeware has advantages in pie baking. It gives pie nice, even, brown undercrust. Glass pans are as safe to use as metal ones if oven temperature is kept slightly lower than called for in recipe.

Overjuicy pies need not run over. Suggestions: Before baking, insert 1½-inch pieces of uncooked macaroni in several of the slits in the top crust. Remove macaroni before serving, of course. Or wrap wet pie tape around the rim before putting the pie in the oven. Or cut the vent slits nearer the center of the top and away from the edges. Or make fluted or forked edge to help seal in the fruit juices. If fruit juice insists on dripping, bake pie on upper rack of oven and catch juices on pan, cookie sheet, or aluminum foil placed in the bottom of the oven. If juices don't run, but you prefer thicker filling, cool pies for 2 or more hours between finishing and serving.

To make fruit pies less juicy, try this: When preparing the filling, beat 1 egg white stiff, mix with the amount of sugar required for the filling, add 1 tablespoonful of flour, then mix thoroughly with fruit and other ingredients, if any.

All that's pie isn't pie-size. Don't forget you can make little pies and tarts too. They're lots of fun and, in a small way, are made the same way as big pies are.

Turnovers made of pie dough are wonderful for picnics and lunch boxes. Cut pie crust in 4-inch squares or 4½-inch circles. Fill half the area with fruit or mince or cheese filling. Turn pastry over to form triangle or half-circle respectively. Seal in filling by pressing the edges together with a fork. Slit the tops and bake 15 minutes at 450° F.

NON-FREEZER REFRIGERATED STORAGE

Two-day-old fruit pies taste oven-fresh if stored in the refrigerator and reheated at 350° F. for 7 to 10 minutes before serving. Pies just brought home from the bakery are also restored to original oven-fresh flavor if heated for about 3 minutes before serving.

Right way to keep pie shells fresh. Pie shells may be made in advance of baking and stored by covering with foil or waxed paper and refrigerated for 2 or 3 days. Or bake pie shells in advance of filling and store, covered; then reheat for 5 minutes at 425° F.

Pie, unless served fresh-from-the-oven warm, must be kept cold. If you don't serve it right after baking, store it in the refrigerator. Once served, whether it came from the oven or refrigerator, don't let pie stand on the table. Slip it right back into the refrigerator.

10

Sweets and Desserts

LOW-COST WAYS TO MAKE NEW DESSERTS, COOKIES, PUDDINGS, AND OTHER TREATS INCLUDING ICE CREAM

Go easy on sugar when you make refrigerator desserts. Too much sugar prevents proper freezing.

Store brown sugar in refrigerator. Moist cold prevents sugar from hardening.

To keep brown sugar soft and moist, place a cut apple or a slice of bread in the container and cover it.

If brown sugar has hardened, rub the solid chunk of sugar back and forth against a kitchen grater placed over a bowl. A kitchen sieve does the trick too.

Store honey in a warm, dry place. If kept in cellar or other damp spot, it is likely to absorb moisture and ferment.

Best way to measure syrups. Thick liquids and syrups (molasses, honey, etc.) should be poured into a measuring cup or spoon from their original containers. If cup has already been used to measure shortening or water, syrup will empty out readily. Don't dip measuring spoon into sticky liquids, for too much will cling to the underside of the spoon, causing overmeasurement or waste.

Measure molasses the easy way. First dip measuring cup full of flour. Empty it back into flour sack (or tin) and you leave a coating that prevents molasses from sticking to the glass. Every drop comes out cleanly.

"A pint a package" is a simple formula to remember for perfect proportion of liquid to prepared puddings and gelatin mixes. For vanilla, chocolate, tapioca, and similar puddings, liquid should be milk. For gelatins, use water or fruit juices.

SOME DESSERT HINTS

Always-fresh doughnuts. To recapture that "just-out-of-the-kettle" flavor of plain cake doughnuts, place them in a covered casserole and bake at 400° F. for 5 minutes. For an added touch of spice that's nice, roll them immediately afterward in sugar-cinnamon mixture.

Mincemeat dumplings. Instead of apple and butter, fill stretched-out biscuits with a cup of prepared mincemeat, reducing sugar to ½ cup.

Gingerbread as an emergency dessert. Keep a package of gingerbread mix on hand and you'll never be caught empty-handed, come dessert time, when you have these topping ideas:

   1. Canned crushed pineapple and whipped cream.

   2. Ice cream covered with chocolate sauce.

   3. Custard sauce and grated orange rind.

   4. Mincemeat folded into whipped cream.

   5. Lemon sauce with nutmeg.

   6. Applesauce sprinkled with sugar and cinnamon, poured on gingerbread, and placed under broiler until sauce bubbles.

   7. A combination of ⅓ cup brown sugar, 2 teaspoons cinnamon, 3 tablespoons butter or margarine, ⅓ cup chopped nuts. Mix well. Sprinkle on top of hot gingerbread, then return it all to the oven for another 5 minutes.

Modern angel cake is heaven-sent, quick, delicious, and easy to make from a packaged angel-cake mix or fresh from the freezer. For an unusual frosting, add instant-coffee powder to heavy cream and whip. Sweeten to taste. For chocolate flavor, add instant cocoa.

No-bake custard. Packaged custard-dessert mix cooks in about 7 minutes, and you cannot tell it from the baked custard in a million years.

Fanciful custards. To maple rennet custard, add teaspoon of sherry. To chocolate custard, add instant-coffee powder, then rum extract. To chocolate custard, add almond extract for exotic flavor.

Cornstarch pudding goes elegant when you make it into black-on-black chocolate pudding by adding a square of melted chocolate. Serve warm, with chocolate ice cream on top.

Dream pudding is simply cornstarch pudding chilled, then beaten with an egg beater and ½ cup whipped heavy cream folded in. Flavor with a dash of almond or rum extract.

Hawaiian pudding is the same old cornstarch pudding, fixed like dream pudding but flavored with vanilla extract and served over pineapple chunks, fresh or thawed frozen.

GELATINS

To loosen gelatins from mold, dip small, pointed knife in warm water and use to loosen firm gelatin from around edge of mold. Then quickly dip mold just to the rim in warm water. Shake mold slightly, cover with serving plate, then invert both plate and mold. Lift off mold.

Value of molds in gelatin desserts. Metal molds not only give the dessert attractive appearance, but, since metal itself chills quickly, dessert becomes firm more quickly than if left in bowl.

Avoid gummy gelatin molds by making sure the powdered gelatin is completely dissolved. Stir all crystal-like particles carefully from sides and bottom of mixing bowl. Keep stirring until completely clear when dipped up in a spoon.

For extra-fast chilling of gelatins, set mold in pan of ice and water. This is a special boon when kitchen time is limited. Also helpful when making layered gelatin molds.

Vary gelatin flavors with liquids. Interesting flavor variation can be created with orange-flavored gelatin. Instead of using full pint of water, mix cup of water with ½ cup grape juice and ½ cup orange juice.

Sink or swim. Some fruits sink, some swim, in gelatin mixtures. These sink: canned apricots, Royal Anne cherries, peaches, pears, pineapple, raspberries; fresh orange sections, grapes; cooked prunes and plums. These float: apple slices and cubes, banana slices, grapefruit sections; fresh peaches, pears, raspberries, strawberry halves; marshmallows and nut meats float too.

Orderly fruit layers. Take advantage of floating and sinking qualities of fruits you combine with gelatin desserts by starting with a layer of sinking kind, then add a layer of the floating kind, and continue until you finish with the sinking kind to hold everything in position, the way you want it.

COOKIES

Mixes make prize packages of mixed cookies. Cookies made from package mixes are always good. They contain finest ingredients and a great variety potential for any cookies you or your recipe book can think of.

In a cookie mix the basic ingredients are in the box of mix. The outside of the box lists simple recipes for making many of your favorite cookie types, such as brownies, refrigerator cookies, crisp cutouts, and so on.

Cake mix makes good cookies too. Did you know that? Try it. Cake-mix manufacturers provide many excellent cookie recipes, often on the cake-mix box.

Add glaze for the professional touch. You can do this before baking, by brushing cookies with cream or egg yolk, or egg white diluted with a little water. Or you can do it after baking, while cookies are still warm, with a sugar glaze mixed from ¾ cup sifted confectioners' sugar and 3 to 4 teaspoons water. Mix until smooth and of frosting consistency, adding a few drops more water if needed.

DROP COOKIES

Grease cookie sheet only lightly, where called for, and only in spots where dough is to be dropped. Allow for spreading, though.

When dropping dough in center of greased spot, use another teaspoon to help you drop mounds of the same size.

If you have no cookie sheet, turn your baking pan upside down, dropping dough on bottom.

Evenly baked cookies depent on heat circulation. That is why your ideal cookie sheet is about 2 inches narrower and shorter than your oven.

If you need an extra cookie sheet, cut aluminum foil the size of your cookie sheet. Cut several pieces. Place foil on sheet, drop cookies on foil. While those are baking, drop dough on another sheet of foil. When the first batch comes out, simply slip off the sheet of baked cookies, slip the cookie sheet under the second piece of foil and cookies, and bake.

Cool cookies on wire racks. Place them next to each other—never overlap or place on top of one another—until they are cool.

STORING COOKIES

Storage. Airtight, cold, or freezing. Store crisp cookies in a container with a loose-fitting cover. To recrisp in humid weather, place cookies in an open shallow pan in a 300° F. oven for 3 to 5 minutes.

Empty butter cartons are fine for molding and storing cookie dough in the refrigerator. The cartons come waxed, so they need no greasing. In addition, when the dough is sliced for cookies, each will be uniform in size.

Refrigerator cookies are refrigerated as dough. Wrap roll of dough in waxed paper or in frozen-juice can from which both end disks have been removed, chill in refrigerator or freezer until dough is firm, then slice and bake the quantity you need.

Cookie doughs are roll-wrapped for freezing the same as for refrigerating, but it's well to overwrap with freezer foil to be sure no moisture is lost during freezing. If roll is difficult to slice when you remove it from the freezer, "thaw" it in the refrigerator for an hour. Freeze drop or roll cookie dough; store in waxed freezer containers or in plastic ones. Thaw before handling, until manageable.

To freeze baked bar and drop cookies, arrange on waxed paper, pack in layers inside a plastic bag or cardboard box. Wrap in freezer paper. You may also use covered, well-sealed plastic boxes. Allow about 15 minutes for thawing.

Other baked cookies are mostly packed in waxed freezer containers or tin boxes with covers. Fill air spaces between cookies with crumpled foil or waxed paper.

Molded cookies are best stored when carefully fitted into cardboard freezer boxes, as they won't break and yet fill box completely.

When sending home-baked cookies to camp or

school, aluminum-foil packing is a smart idea. Being greaseproof, odorproof, and moistureproof, foil insures that the cookies (or cake) arrive in perfect condition, moist and fresh. And since aluminum is in the nature of a soft suit of armor, your baking will arrive unbroken and uncrushed if packed right, with air spaces properly filled.

ICE CREAM AT YOUR FINGERTIPS

You can make ice cream in a crank freezer, hand or electric. Let's see how it works with banana ice cream. Mix together 2 cups mashed ripe bananas (made from 5 or 6 bananas), 1½ tablespoons lemon juice, ½ cup granulated sugar. Add ½ teaspoon salt, 2 beaten eggs, 1 cup milk, 1½ teaspoons vanilla extract. Stir in 2 cups heavy cream. Freeze in 2-quart freezer until it becomes hard to crank, using 8 parts ice to 1 part ice-cream salt. Makes 2 quarts.

Make ice cream in your refrigerator ice-cube tray too. Take peach ice cream as an example. Turn refrigerator temperature control to coldest setting. Then combine ⅔ cup canned sweet condensed milk, ½ cup cold water, ⅛ teaspoon salt, 1½ teaspoons vanilla extract. Add 2 cups sieved fresh or thawed frozen peaches, 1 or 2 drops of almond extract, 1 teaspoon lemon juice. Refrigerate. Whip 1 cup heavy cream to custardlike consistency, then fold into chilled mixture. Turn into chilled bowl. With egg beater or electric mixer, beat until smooth but not melted. Quickly fill freezer tray and freeze until firm. Makes about 6 servings.

Use package pudding to make ice cream. Pick your flavor. To package of gelatin prepared pudding add ¼ cup sugar and a dash of salt. Chill. Fold in cup of heavy cream, whippped. Turn into freezer tray and freeze for 1 hour at coldest refrigerator temperature. Turn into bowl, beat with an egg beater until smooth but not melted. Return to tray, freeze until firm, about 3 or 4 hours. Makes 1 quart.

Ice cream is sensitive. It loses most of its velvety texture if handled too much. The richer the cream, the colder is the freezing and storing temperature it requires, especially for long storage. Ice-cream desserts need low temperatures even more. Unless stored at zero freezer temperature, don't keep ice cream longer than a few hours.

Who wants to wait for ice cream? When the ice-cream carton is hard to pull off, just cut through the rim with a knife and your ice cream is ready to serve.

Ice cream is good for a month in your home freezer, if you follow the instructions you received with your freezer on storing ice cream.

Store unopened containers of ice cream in the coldest section of your freezer. To keep·at serving consistency, store one or two cartons away from the freezing coils or in the special ice-cream compartments that modern freezers provide. Opened cartons are best covered by a double thickness of cellophane first, then tightly resealed to avoid loss of flavor and the formation of ice crystals.

In refrigerator-freezer combinations the normal setting is zero, just right for storing ice-cream desserts hours ahead. The freezer part of the combination can be set at coldest point without affecting the temperature of the refrigerator itself.

11

Fruits and Jellies

LITTLE-KNOWN TIPS TO SAVE MONEY, WORK, AND TIME

Fruits are one of those foods that are both delicious and nutritious, and few people need persuading to eat them. But why not consider some new and less familiar kinds along with your favorites? As with so many food items today, the consumer has a wide choice of fruits throughout the year (and when the fresh aren't to be had, there are always canned fruits). The only drawback with modern methods of distributing fresh produce is that, in concentrating on varieties that transport well and survive long, we have sacrificed flavor and texture. But you can still have the best of both worlds if you take the trouble to learn when the best local fruits and imported varieties are on the stands and in the stores. Learn the names of the varieties and the sources of the fruit you find best, make a list, and then hold out each year until these are available. Resist buying the "first of the season"—unless you know they are truly good—for you will pay dearly for the privilege.

Save time when peeling pears or peaches. First scald the fruit with boiling water, then peel. Skins come off much easier that way.

Apple to the rescue. A slice of apple added to each

pint of cranberries before cooking will greatly improve the flavor without sacrificing any of the tartness.

Place a cut apple in your cookie jar or fruitcake box. It will keep soft cookies soft and fruitcake moist. Caution: don't store apples with crisp cookies.

Leftover fruit juices have many uses. They make fruit gelatin desserts more fruity, and they can "make" the sauce you pour over ice cream, pudding, or cake. They improve the tang of French dressing. Fruit syrup has same usefulness. Also, try mixing it into mayonnaise or with cream cheese.

Leftover fruit goes over big when added to chilled summer drinks, when found atop a mound of dish dessert, when crushed into cake-drenching sauce, when used mixed in gelatin, when mixed with peanut butter as sandwich filling.

Salt enhances sweet flavors. Proper function of salt is to develop and bring out natural food flavors, not to make foods taste salty. Sprinkle small amount in fruit juices; it decreases sourness of acids and increases sweetness of sugars.

CITRUS FRUITS

To keep lemons, limes, oranges fresh, wrap them in tissue or oiled paper and keep them in dry, cool place or on low shelf in refrigerator. Or keep them in a closed fruit jar in refrigerator.

To keep lemons for months, after you buy them at a bargain, put the whole lemons into sterilized canning jars, cover with cold water, adjust rubber rings, and screw covers down tightly. Not only will they stay fresh for months, they will yield much more juice than when you first bought them.

Get more juice. Even when you do no long-term storing you get more juice from lemons, limes, and oranges if you soak them in a pan of water for a while before squeezing. Then, before cutting, roll the fruit around on the table with your hand.

Citrus bonus. For more flavorful fresh-fruit drinks, place orange and lemon rind in cold water so that rind is fully covered. Bring to boiling point. Remove rinds. Add fruit-flavored cooking water to fruit juices.

Strain without strain. Moisten cheesecloth in water and wrap around end of lemon. Juice will strain-as-you-squeeze.

Lemon-aid in fruit chopping. Before you chop sticky fruits, put a few drops of lemon juice into the food to be chopped. Makes cleaning easy.

Beat life into canned orange juice. Wonder why canned orange juice may lack that "fresh-squeezed" taste? It's because, during canning, air is removed. That's why economical canned orange juice should be stirred vigorously, or aerated, with a rotary beater, an electric blender, or poured several times between two containers.

To peel an orange without spattering, dig heel of paring knife into skin and draw it backward around middle of orange. Then insert smooth teaspoon handle into the cut and work it around until you pry the skin loose. Remove one half at a time.

When grating rind of lemon or orange, be sure not to grate too deep. The colored part of rind gives the flavor while the white part causes food to taste bitter.

For trim orange or grapefruit sections, set fruit on board; then, with a sharp knife, whittle off peel in strips, cutting from top to bottom and deep enough to remove all white membrane. Next cut along both sides of such dividing membrane and lift out each section. Work over a bowl at this point, so you save all the juice.

COOLING AND FREEZING FRUITS

Fresh berries. Spread berries out on tray and store in refrigerator on an open sheet. Chill, but do not wash until shortly before using. Then place in colander and run cold water gently over berries. If there are hulls, remove after washing, to save flavor.

Keep strawberries firm even if you must store them several days before using. Put them in the refrigerator in a colander. The cold air, circulating through the berries, will keep them firm and fresh.

Cold, but not too cold. To enjoy its full flavor, remove fruit from refrigerator a little ahead of serving, so that it can warm up a bit. (Remember not to store bananas in the refrigerator.)

Before freezing berries or cherries, wash them in ice-cold water. Better results, less waste.

Prevent darkening of fruits. For those fruits that have a tendency to darken in freezing, add ¼ teaspoon ascorbic acid (vitamin C) to each cup of syrup. You can buy the ascorbic acid at the drugstore.

During fresh-fruit season, freeze fruit in half-pint containers, for lunches at later date. Consult your Agricultural Extension literature on how to freeze fruits.

When thawing time is short, put unopened carton of quick-frozen fruit in a bowl of water and let it stand about 25 minutes. Fruit will be thawed and ready to serve when you open the container.

Frozen fruit looks best, tastes best if served when just thawed, while there are still a few ice crystals left.

SOME ANSWERS TO JELLY-MAKING

Tough jelly? Probably you are using too little sugar to balance the recipe proportions.

To keep fruit from floating in jam, use fully ripened fruit, crush it thoroughly, cook sufficiently, and, when ready, cool and stir for 5 minutes before filling jars. Skim foam from top and stir thoroughly, then fill jars.

When jelly will not jell, place the glasses in the oven, at 250° F., for about an hour. This saves the time and effort needed to remove the jelly from jars and reboil and does the trick just as nicely.

Jelly gets cloudy if poured too slowly or too late (jelly has started to form and particles hold tiny air bubbles), juice is pulpy (avoid this by straining through clean, wet jelly bag), setting is premature because recipe has not been followed carefully and accurately.

Mold forms on jelly if imperfectly sealed. You can cut out mold and use remainder of jelly, since mold does not penetrate below the surface of the jelly. Or do this: pour ¼ teaspoon brandy or grain alcohol over jelly, roll glass so liquid covers the entire surface, then light it. When alcohol has burned off, mold is gone. Apply new coating of paraffin at once.

If homemade jelly changes color, here's the possible reason: darkening at top is caused by air getting through paraffin. You then need tin or paper covers in addition to paraffin. Fading, especially in berries, occurs if jelly is not stored in cool, dark place.

What makes jelly "weep?" Unbalanced recipe, with surplus acid (possible with high sugar solids in original juice), too-heavy layer of paraffin (⅛-inch layer offers best protection), too-warm storage (keep below 65° F.), changes in temperature.

Syrupy jelly is caused when there is too little pectin, acid, or sugar to balance the proportions.

Crystals in jelly, caused by any of these: too much sugar, too slow or too long cooking (evaporation), too little cooking (insufficient inversion of sugar), evaporation due to uncovered jelly.

Too-stiff jellies result from overbalance of pectin or sugar in mixture. Happens when fruit is not fully ripe or when overcooking causes excessive evaporation. Latter can be avoided by boiling at high heat and cooking quickly.

Gummy jelly is caused by overcooking. Acid may affect the action of pectin.

12

Beverages

COFFEE, TEA, CHOCOLATE, AND OTHER LIGHT DRINKS TO REFRESH YOUR TASTE AND BUDGET

Tired of the same old tricks? Why not start today to experiment with different brands, varieties, and beverages. There are far more choices available even on supermarket shelves than the standard kinds. Some may cost a bit more, but some cost less: over the long run, they shouldn't add that much to your budget, and you'll certainly get more pleasure out of what you do drink.

COFFEE

Most of the coffee we drink comes from only a few places, even though the standard brands are usually blends. But there are many different coffee beans grown around the world. Even with the commercially available standard brands, you can make your own blends. For instance, next time you go to brew a pot, use a teaspoon or two less of your regular brand and substitute the equivalent of one of the espresso brands. These are darker, finer ground, and have a slightly different taste. See if you like what it does to your regular coffee. If you don't, try other combinations.

True coffee connoisseurs will insist that the only way to get good coffee is to start with the freshly roasted bean. Specialty stores often sell a variety of coffee beans —expensive, perhaps, but worth trying. Then some of the large supermarket chains still sell the beans that they can grind to order. These are often cheaper.

Or you can grind your own at home. Only the purest of the pure insist on grinding coffee by hand. There are several fine electric grinders that do the essential job: provide fresh coffee in the exact quantity as you want it.

An electric coffee grinder holds a pound of bean coffee. If you keep a spare pound on hand, you're always prepared to make perfect coffee. Beans keep best in the refrigerator or freezer, but short-time shelf storage is satisfactory too.

If you don't want to be bothered with searching for different beans or grinding your own, at least keep what you do buy as fresh as possible. Once exposed to the air, coffee tends to go stale in about 10 days. Two rules for keeping vacuum-packed coffee fresh: Seal the lid tightly after withdrawing coffee to use. Keep the closed container in your refrigerator. If lid is bent or hard to tamp down tightly, try using a jar for coffee storage. The lid is easier to turn tight.

Everyone has the secret for making the best cup of coffee—yet somehow everyone has a different secret. Experiment and find your own way. Unfortunately, too much experimentation would involve too many different and expensive kinds of equipment. So use the coffeemaker you have and see if you can produce more desirable results by varying amounts of coffee or water, cooking longer or shorter periods, mixing blends as suggested.

A clean pot makes good coffee. One thing everyone

agrees on: the coffeepot should be cleaned of old coffee oils, stains, and any other remains. Run your automatic coffeemaker through a perking or other brewing cycle occasionally when you've put water and baking soda in the pot. Clean it thoroughly afterward with clear water to be sure no trace of the taste of soda remains inside the pot.

Fill it with cold water between brewings if you use your automatic coffeemaker every day. Water absorbs unwanted odors and flavors that may develop in the coffeemaker if stored dry.

Plug your coffeemaker, filled with water and coffee, into your range timer outlet or into a similar outlet of a wake-up-to-music radio at night; set the timer a little earlier than you get up in the morning and you can have coffee waiting when you wake up.

The new drip coffeemakers undoubtedly leave the least grounds and sludge. And if you are able to buy the newer and better models, you now have considerable control over the strength of the coffee you make. One drawback for the budget is the constant expense of buying filters. But look in the papers or magazines, or inquire around and find where you can buy the standard filters in large quantities at considerably less cost.

One cup of coffee coming up, in a hurry. Why bother brewing even in a 2-cup pot when boiling water and a spoon is all you need for a quick cup of excellent coffee made with instant powdered coffee? There are a wide variety of brands to choose from, and the "freeze-dried" do seem to produce a more natural coffee taste. If you know that you are going to be drinking instant coffee steadily, buy in as large a quantity as reasonable, because you pay a disproportionate sum for the small sizes.

Use instant coffee in your coffeemaker, too. Simply make the number of cups you want, in quantity in the coffeemaker, with spares for seconds, and serve from the coffeemaker instead of making individual servings in coffee cups.

Coffee substitutes taste much like coffee and are available for people for whom coffee is too stimulating or who are on special diets that do not include coffee.

Decaffeinated coffee. This is true coffee, but with most of the caffein, the part that stimulates, taken out. It's also for people who can't drink coffee. Brew it just as you do coffee.

TEA

As with coffee, there are far more varieties available even on supermarket shelves than most people realize. Unless you are absolutely positive you have found your tea-of-paradise, try some of the different kinds. You may be in for some pleasant surprises, teas that will turn a routine cup into a delightful experience.

In addition to the classic teas, there are the herb teas. Many peoples around the world drink them, and in recent years they have become more widely appreciated and available here. Some are imported, but others are domestic, and if they cost more than standard brands you may find yourself drinking less but enjoying it more. And even if they don't have all the medicinal or health properties claimed by some, they at least provide a pleasant change.

A good cup of tea. Personal preferences vary widely, but there are general rules for making good tea:

When kettle water boils, pour a cup of water into a china or earthenware teapot. (Glass is a good teapot material too.) Let stand for a minute, to warm pot, then empty out the heating water.

Measure desired amount of tea leaves (2 teaspoonfuls of tea leaves to 2½ cups of water is medium strength) into heated teapot. Pour freshly boiling water over the leaves and let steep 2 to 3 minutes before serving.

Weaker tea for special tastes. Never dilute the tea in the pot. Instead add hot water to individual cups of tea or provide hot water in a container so a guest or member of your family may help himself.

Real tea connoisseurs abhor the tea bag, but it's undoubtedly a convenience. Just don't serve a cup of hot water with a bag on the side. Instead pour hot water over the bag, in the cup, and allow the drinker to decide when to remove the tea bag.

You can use tea bags in the teapot too. Follow directions for making tea with leaves, and remove bags before serving tea, after tea has steeped as directed. An occasional swish as tea steeps will give you full strength from the bags.

Tea sensation. Next time you serve tea with lemon, stick a small clove into each side of the lemon slice. Changes a taken-for-granted beverage into something really special.

CHOCOLATE

Chocolate or cocoa? Both are derived from the seeds of Theobroma cacao, a tropical evergreen tree. Some of the fat is extracted from chocolate to make cocoa.

You can buy chocolate in solid form unsweetened and semi-sweet. Chocolate bits may also be melted and used, with milk, to make hot chocolate. And always add a dash of salt.

Cocoa's easy to make because it comes combined with sugar and dried milk, so that all you need to add is boiling water. For richer cocoa, make it with hot milk or combine cocoa and milk and heat together, stirring until it almost reaches the boiling point.

Iced mint cocoa. Make cocoa as usual, increasing sugar for sweet tooths. Strain hot cocoa and chill. When cold add 1 teaspoon vanilla and pour into tall glasses partially filled with crushed ice. Top each glass with whipped cream and garnish with mint leaves.

Iced chocolate mocha. Combine 1 cup strong hot coffee, 3 cups milk, and ½ cup chocolate syrup. Beat with egg beater or electric mixer until frothy. Pour over ice in medium-sized glasses, with whipped cream on top.

COOL DRINKS FOR HOT DAYS

Sugar syrup. This is a very convenient commodity to have in your refrigerator during cold-drink time since it dissolves, whereas granulated sugar does not do so readily. Simply boil any quantity you want of equal amounts of sugar and water. Stir only until sugar dissolves. Boil it for 10 minutes. Pour into a sterilized jar, cover, and keep chilled in your refrigerator.

Warm-weather fruit drinks need not go flat. Avoid weakening their flavors with ice cubes by adding some of the beverage itself (lemonade, etc.) to the water in your ice-cube tray before freezing the cubes.

Ice cubes for vacuum bottle. To manufacture ice cubes that will fit into the mouth of vacuum bottles, fold long strips of heavy waxed paper into pleats (perhaps milk-container cardboard) and slip the paper into the tray after filling it with water. When frozen, dislodge the cubes by pulling the pleated section apart. (Also gives novel touch to highballs and cocktails.)

Rhubarb flip. Stir 1 cup sweetened rhubarb juice, 1 tablespoon sugar, and a dash of nutmeg into 3 well-beaten egg yolks. Pour over cracked ice in tall glasses. Fill with ginger ale.

Tea punch. Tea is a wonderful extender for punches. Use it many ways. Here's one idea: to 1 cup strong tea infusion add 1 cup sweetened strawberry juice, ½ cup orange juice, and 3 tablespoons lemon juice. Chill. Just before serving, add 1 cup chilled dry ginger ale. Pour into chilled glasses and garnish with whole berries.

Rhubarb tea punch is another recipe using cold tea. Add 6 tablespoons lemon juice, ½ cup sugar, small bunch fresh mint, two cups slightly sweetened stewed rhubarb, and a stick of cinnamon to 1 cup of tea. Chill. When ready to serve, remove cinnamon and add 1 quart cracked ice, 1 sliced orange, 1 quart chilled ginger ale, and 1 pint iced carbonated water. Serve with straws in tall glasses.

Lemonade for one. Allow the juice of 1 lemon for a tall glass of lemonade, add sugar syrup to taste, and fill a glass half full of ice with either water or soda water.

Frozen lemonade is fine for people who like their lemonade pleasantly sweetened. It tastes like lemonade made from fresh lemons.

Make orangeade with frozen concentrated orange juice. Turn orange juice into orangeade by simply combining the 1 can concentrate and 3 cans water with the juice of a lemon or two and serving it over ice in tall glasses.

13

Sandwiches,
Box Lunches,
Picnics, and Cookouts

SOME TREATS AND TIPS FOR
ADDING VARIETY TO
INFORMAL MEALS

Sandwich bread should not be too fresh, or it may tear when spread with butter or fillings. Day-old bread is best. And remember, many bake shops and supermarkets feature day-old bread at reduced prices. (It comes out of the freezer like fresh-baked bread, too, after sandwich thaws.)

For neat sandwiches, lay out bread slices so that those next to each other in orginal loaf (same size) can be paired together. This makes cutting, wrapping, and eating easier.

Avoid monotony in sandwich making. Vary the breads, or even combine slices of different kinds in one sandwich. Rolls or fancy breads also make a nice change. Try cheese bread and raisin bread in the same sandwich.

Ways to grill sandwiches. Butter bottom of lower

slice and top of upper slice of bread. Put filling between slices. Toast in broiler, turning once, in electric
grill, or toast in skillet, turning with pancake turner. Or
toast, unbuttered, under broiler; or in electric toaster
by the slice. Tuck in lettuce after grilling.

Storage tip on sandwich fillings. Keep ground meat
and other ground fillings in covered jars in refrigerator.
Use within 2 to 4 days. Tart fillings keep better than
mild ones. Ground meat, cooked or uncooked, does
not keep as well as sliced meat.

PACK-IN-THE-BOX

Freezer can be box-lunch paradise. Since sandwiches
may be stored in the freezer from 2 to 3 weeks, you
can make them when you have time, not be plagued by
last-minute rush. Nix on hard-cooked eggs, though.
(They deteriorate when frozen.)

If several sandwiches of same kind are to be stored
in your freezer, after wrapping in moisture-vaporproof
material, pack either in top-opening waxed cartons
(properly labeled), in metal refrigerator trays with
covers, or in plastic bag with top twisted, gooseneck
fashion, and secured with string or rubber band.

Pack sandwiches from freezer straight into lunch
box. They will thaw in about 3 hours, just in time for
lunch.

Like fresh sandwiches? To keep them that way, after
you've wrapped them, press the ends of the waxed
paper together with a hot iron. Keeps them about as
fresh as when you made them.

Pack lettuce separately for freezer sandwiches for
picnics. But for lunch boxes tuck lettuce into frozen
sandwiches and rewrap. Lettuce will stay nice and
crisp as the sandwich thaws. You could do the same
for picnics, but why do all the work when people can
help themselves at a picnic?

For families in which several carry lunches, preparation time can be cut considerably by the assembly-line method. Lay out bread for all sandwiches to be filled in a double row of bread slices. Spread filling in one operation down one line of bread; butter, margarine, or mayonnaise down the second line. Put them together, with lettuce if they're to be eaten that day, without if you're making sandwiches for the freezer.

Household aluminum foil does as well in lunch box as in refrigerator or in cooking. Perfect for wrapping irregularly shaped foods. Can be reused if handled carefully.

Disposable containers for lunch box are especially good for person who does not wish to carry containers home. Inexpensive wax-paper bags, waxed cups, and paper spoons, forks, etc., are easily disposable.

PICNIC TIPS

Afraid to pack ice in picnic basket? Here's a way to keep melting ice from ruining your carefully made picnic-food plans: Fill empty, rinsed milk carton with cold water the day before. Reseal opening carefully. Freeze solid in your home freezer or refrigerator, but leave a 2-inch space at the top of the carton, for water expands when it freezes. Put carton in your picnic box. Even when ice finally melts in carton, it won't drip, for the carton remains sealed.

Why not use that ice? You won't be unpacking your lunch until you're ready to eat, so why not bring along an ice pick when you picnic, chop up the ice in the milk carton (easy to get at by simply slitting the carton away from the ice with a sharp knife you bring along too) and use it to cool the drinks you bring along?

Ice in double boiler? If you want your salads to taste fresh at the picnic, pack them in a double boiler with ice in the bottom container.

Cover of thermos jug stuck? Instead of fretting, insure against it. Before you use jug again, spread a bit of fresh shortening or salad oil over thread of cap. Caution: wash cap after each use, because fat or oil might become rancid.

Ants are allergic to chalk. When going on a picnic, take along a piece of soft white chalk. Use it to draw a heavy mark around edges of picnic table. This magic circle will repel any of the bold crawlers from making their way up the table.

COOKOUT HINTS

Oven shelf for grill. The wire shelf from your oven makes a marvelous picnic stove. Support the corners over the fire with stones or tin cans. It will hold your skillet or frying pan and prove ideal for broiling beef or grilling frankfurters.

Quick-brick picnic fire. To get a quick blaze when you build a picnic fire, soak an unglazed brick in kerosene for a day or two before you plan your outing. The brick will start your fire immediately, will ignite damp logs without kindling, and burn for quite a while on the kerosene fuel alone.

Wear wet gloves in outdoor cookery. Next time you have picnic or outdoor barbecue, have pair of canvas work gloves handy. Soaked in water, they're almost as good as asbestos to prevent hand burns.

Chefs keep a cool head in the hot sun. Line your hat with aluminum foil. Slip edges of foil under sweatband to avoid actual contact with hair or skin.

To roast wienies safely, take along a few extra paper plates and impale them on roasting fork up around edge of handle. They protect hand from scorching heat of fire. Remember, they're made of paper, so don't get them too close to heat.

It's easy to cook chicken on an outdoor grill. Just place chicken (cut into frying-size pieces), mushrooms, and seasonings on a large square of foil. Seal into a tight packet and cook on grate over hot coals. Frozen vegetables with seasonings and butter added may be cooked in same manner.

14

A Bouquet of Herbs

APPLIED PROPERLY, THESE TURN FLAT MEALS INTO PLEASURABLE EXPERIENCES

Herbs are but one of many types of seasoning available—seasonings that range from the familiar salt, pepper, cloves, vanilla, mustard, and garlic to the more exotic such as curry powder, tabasco sauce, or saffron. Since it is assumed that most people already have some experience and preferences in using most of the other seasonings, and since a certain mystique has developed around cooking with herbs, a few hints about their use should set people at ease.

To be used most effectively, herbs must be applied subtly. You may want to experiment, but the general rule is to use small quantities. A basic measure is ¼ teaspoon dried or crushed herbs or 1 teaspoon chopped fresh ones in a dish to serve four persons.

Fresh herbs, in most cases, definitely are preferable to dried herbs. If you can't buy them fresh, consider growing them at home yourself. Any competent gardener can do so by planting in a sunny plot with good drainage. You might even consider growing them in pots—and indoors. Read up on this in a reputable book: one taste of your own fresh parsley, basil, or chives will make it worthwhile.

Herbs can add magic to your meals. Chives pep up cottage cheese, bay leaf is a natural for chicken or pea soup, chopped parsley enhances a boiled new potato, and your own inventiveness will carry you from experimentation with herbs to a sure touch.

When gravy isn't just gravy. Add a sprinkle of dried dill and stir vigorously. It's a treat all by itself.

An easy trick is to tie together several large sprigs of parsley, a small sprig of tarragon, and one of thyme. Then drop this herb bouquet into a kettle of soup, stew, any meat or fowl dish that is cooked with moist heat. Or try putting an herb bouquet into the cavity of a roasting chicken. It does wonderful things to the flavor of the meat besides eliminating the necessity for stuffing the fowl.

BASIC HERB GUIDE

Basil. This is a easy-to-grow herb with a clover-bloom-like flavor. Use it in any recipe that calls for tomatoes, sprinkle into a green salad or scrambled eggs.

Bay leaf. The versatile leaf with really pungent flavor. Add to home-made vegetable soup, chicken dishes, pea soup, cooking water of beets, onions, and potatoes. Crush and add to tomato juice, soup, or aspic.

Borage. Good only in its fresh form (and its young leaves can even be cooked and served like spinach), this herb provides a subtle, cucumberlike flavor for such delicacies as aspics or fish sauces. It is also used traditionally in punches or lemonades.

Burnet. Like borage, this has a cucumberish flavor and also should be used fresh. Only the tender young center leaves are suitable, but the seeds may be soaked in vinegar that is then used in salad dressings.

Capers. These tiny buds of the caper bush have the sharp taste of a gherkin and add a piquant touch to many a dish. They are especially common in tartar sauce.

Caraway. Both the leaves and seeds of this herb are commonly used, the former in soups and stews, the latter on rye bread, sauerkraut, cheeses, borsch, and in marinades. But never cook the seeds too long with any dish or they become bitter. Used in salads or with vegetables, the seeds should be crushed first to release the flavor.

Chervil. This is a delicate herb that resembles parsley. It goes well with omelets, green salads, Welsh rarebits, cheese spreads, and in the melted butter you pour over green vegetables. Use it, too, on chicken, before broiling.

Chives. Mildest of the onion family, chives are superb in cold potato soup, vichyssoise; potato, fish, and vegetable salads. They blend with cheese for appetizer dip and as a sandwich spread, make a perfect topping, chopped, over cream or clear soups. Stir into cream sauce, omelet, lemon-butter sauce.

Coriander. Only the fresh leaves are used—not the stem—and the whole leaf is placed in soups such as pea or chicken, in stews, or on top of roasts. The seed is also used in such dishes as gingerbread, apple pie, or curry, where its "bite" will not overpower.

Cumin. This is one of the basic herbs of Indian curry powder, but it is also used alone in other foods— cheeses, baked dishes, eggs, beans, rice-dishes, chilis, tomato sauces. When it is called for in reputable recipes, try it as directed.

Dill. This herb has feathery green leaves, has a flavor that adds piquancy to many a dish. Add to melted butter as a dip for lobster, crabmeat, or shrimp. Stir into cream or cottage cheese, mashed potatoes. Toss with green, potato, fish, or vegetable salads.

Garlic. Another member of the onion family, garlic has a bad reputation in some quarters. In fact, used properly, it is a fine addition to many foods and is in no way overpowering. Rub a wooden salad bowl with a cut clove of garlic. Soak some cloves in salad dressings if you prefer. Place slivers on meat as it is being cooked, add cloves to stews or sauces. Above all, use fresh garlic whenever possible.

Marjoram. Sweet-smelling as a flower, it's a must on any herb shelf. Use with veal cutlet or Swiss steak. Rub over beef, lamb, or pork before roasting. Add to cheese dishes, omelet, green or vegetable salads, meat loaf, meat pie, stew. Toss with stuffing for chicken or fish.

Oregano. A "natural" with tomatoes. Mix with sauce for spaghetti dishes, add to tomato sauce or soup, meat casseroles. Rub over pork, lamb, or veal before roasting. Use in potato or fish salad.

Parsley. This is certainly one of the most common herbs, flavorful in itself and useful for blending the flavors of other herbs. The stems as well as leaves (even the roots of some of the many varieties available) are used in a wide range of dishes—soups, salads, meats. Aside from its taste, parsley is also rich in protein.

Rosemary. A delicate and versatile herb that has many flavoring possibilities. Add to pan when roasting beef, lamb, pork, or veal. Sprinkle lightly inside poultry before stuffing. Mix into biscuit or dumpling dough before cooking or baking, to serve with meat. Use in stew or meat loaf. Add to water when cooking peas, potatoes, spinach, turnips.

Saffron. Known mainly for the golden orange color it imparts to rice or other dishes, saffron may also be used for flavoring dressings, cakes, or breads. Use only the small amounts called for in recipes. Saffron, by the way, is the stigma of the autumn crocus.

Sage. Used sparingly, sage adds a welcome flavor to cheeses, chowders, omelets, pork, sausage, duck, or goose. The freshly chopped leaves are far superior to the dried form.

Savory. This herb has a spicy flavor. Use in any dish made with dried peas, beans, or lentils. Mix in stuffing, ground beef, gravy, stew, croquettes, green salad, scrambled eggs, omelet. Sprinkle over baked or broiled fish just before serving.

Tarragon. A tangy and sharp herb that is good chopped for tartare and lemon-butter sauces. Add to fish or egg salads. Toss with green salad or stir into the dressing. Blend with butter to pour over broiled steak or vegetables. Sprinkle over cottage-cheese salad.

Thyme. An aromatic herb that's meant for poultry, meat, and fish stuffing. Add it to dishes made with tomato or cheese. Sprinkle over tomato-clam chowder. Add to meat stew or pot roast. Combine with melted butter to serve over vegetables.

15

The Home Freezer

WAYS TO SAVE MONEY, FOOD, AND TIME WITH THIS STORAGE CONVENIENCE

Money-saver. You can buy for the freezer when your favorite supermarket or food store runs specials when seasonal large supplies bring prices down. You can often buy in quantity at discount prices. Stow away scraps of this and that until you have enough to make low-cost stews and casseroles.

Better food. Because, on the whole, you buy when prices are in your favor, you can now buy only the best food.

Best food in season and out. Because many foods store as long as a year, you can have strawberries in February, garden-fresh asparagus in November, an oyster cocktail in July. You can eat trout, salmon, and venison—not only after a fishing or hunting expedition, but any time during the year.

Time-saver. With a home freezer you can buy enough and store enough prepared foods at one time to yield up a complete meal at a moment's notice to-day—not just for the family but for unexpected guests as well—tomorrow, and day after day.

Work-saver. With a home freezer your cooking side of housekeeping is lightened. You need not shell peas, scrape carrots, or soak spinach in a hurry once the freezer is stocked with foods that need only to be brought to the range and cooked, or thawed and eaten.

No more worries. Whether you're late coming back from a downtown shopping trip or company drops in out of the blue, you're saved by the freezer. All you have to do is reach into it and pull out any kind and quantity of the delicious food you like.

Prepare party foods ahead. Why be tired out when your guests arrive if you can have the party food in the freezer days or even weeks before the big day?

If you're without power, your home freezer will hold foods as long as two days if you don't open the door or lid. Longer power delays are rare. But if they occur, dry ice placed on top of frozen foods will keep them in frozen state still longer.

MANAGING YOUR FREEZER

Freezer management will be more successfully experienced if you proceed gradually. Don't, for instance, fill the freezer with the first products of the season. As the year passes you'll want to add many things. As a guide to help you decide how much space to reserve for various foods, 1 cubic foot will hold about 40 pint cartons or about 35 to 40 pounds of meat (not including whole poultry).

For best results, freeze only specified amounts for the size of your freezer at one time. The use-and-care book which comes with the appliance will give you this information.

Freeze foods as fast as possible. To do this, be sure they are in contact with the sides of a freezer chest or on the permanent refrigerated shelves of your upright freezer.

Once food is frozen you can store it anywhere within the freezer, thus freeing the refrigerated walls or shelves for further freezing.

Organizing your freezer, with special sections for meat, fruit, vegetables, breads, and desserts, simplifies finding items quickly when you are planning a freezer meal. You might also like to have separate storage sections for beef, lamb, poultry, and so forth.

Some combined meals, sometimes called TV dinners, can be stored together for unexpected dinner guests, school lunches, or special diets.

Package carefully to be sure there's as little air as possible between contents and covering, using moisture-vaporproof materials.

Packages should be labeled as to content and date. Since foods have maximum storage time, arrange foods that have been in the freezer the longest time on top and near the front of your freezer.

Reorganize as you shop and add new freezer foods, so you'll keep freezer packages coming out in about the order they went in.

Use your freezer for day-to-day meals so that frozen foods are in prime condition when they become part of your menus.

You'll want to keep an inventory to help you remember quantities of various foods and length of time they've been in your freezer. Keep the record accurate so you'll know when to replenish supplies as well as when to use up foods that have reached their time limit in the frozen state.

If you experiment with prepared foods for the freezer, keep a record of the method you used. If it was satisfactory, you can repeat the method; if not, you will try to improve your method.

Take your pick of record keepers. An inventory list on a blackboard near the freezer, with a magnetized pencil that sticks to the metal board; a record book, a card file, a calendar—these are all good ways to keep track of just what you have in your freezer.

A FEW FREEZING DO'S
AND DON'T'S

Do use your use-and-care booklet. It can guide you toward best use of your home freezer.

Don't use more than you need. If you want to cook only part of a package of frozen food, remove one end of the package with a sharp knife. (There are special knives made for cutting frozen foods.) Cover the exposed end of remaining frozen food with moisture-vaporproof material and return to the freezer.

To thaw or not to thaw is often the question. Most vegetables should be cooked from the solid state (corn on the cob is an exception). If in doubt, read package directions.

Package family-size servings. Small packages freeze and thaw more quickly than do larger ones.

Always package foods that are to be layered, such as hamburgers, with two thickness of packaging material between the layers, so they can be separated easily when frozen.

Cover sharp bones, or other protruding parts that might tear wrapping, with extra patches of material, for extra strength.

Leave head space in containers, especially for liquids, for expansion during freezing. Follow manufacturer's directions and use minimum amount of head space recommended, because air permits dehydration and damages frozen-food quality.

Trap those odors. Be sure that smoked meats, especially, are completely covered and sealed before freezing them. Leaking odors could permeate other foods in the freezer.

Fruit floats? Hold it down with a crushed piece of moisture-vaporproof material between carton contents and cover. This prevents discoloration and flavor loss of fruit.

Wrap fruit pies after you freeze them. This makes them easier to handle. Don't delay the wrapping, though, or pie will deteriorate in quality.

Label all food carefully. There are several types of inks and pencils on the market for labeling. A china marking pencil or crayon is fine for labeling glass and plastic containers.

Don't refreeze quick-frozen foods once they've thawed. There's usually a loss of quality when thawed foods are frozen, so use them promptly.

When freezing cooked foods, cool them as quickly as possible after cooking. Then package and freeze at once.

Seasonings are fine, but use of some in freezing foods is inadvisable. Onions and sage gradually lose flavor during freezer storage. Cloves and garlic become stronger. Plan to add most seasonings when reheating the food.

Avoid freezing fried foods. They're apt to become rancid even after a very short storage period.

DEFROSTING

Twice a year is usually often enough to defrost your freezer. It isn't even necessary to shut off the motor. Simply remove the contents, if possible, when you have plenty of room in your refrigerator, and scrape off the frost with a blunt instrument.

Defrost when stocks are low if you want to do a thorough cleaning job within your freezer.

A quick way to melt freezer frost in a horizontal-type machine is to remove all contents, pull the plug, and blow warm air inside with your vacuum-cleaner hose attached at the blowing end. Close the lid on the hose (it's rugged enough to take this for 15 minutes) and the warm air will soon melt the frost. After that you simply sponge out the water into a basin, clean the interior with water and baking soda, rinse with clear water, and wipe dry. Plug it back in and replace frozen foods after the temperature is well below freezing (32° F.).

16

Kitchen Appliances

RANGES, REFRIGERATORS, AND ELECTRICAL APPLIANCES THAT MAKE MEAL PREPARATION EASIER AND MORE PLEASANT

If you're buying a new range, ask about the new surface units that turn the heat down automatically after foods begin to cook. Initial range cost is a little higher than for those not equipped with these units, but you'll have years of economical and carefree cooking if you buy the latest convenience that does some of your work for you.

Your gas-range pilot light is most efficient if you regulate the flame height until it is blue with just a trace of yellow at the top. And keep assembly clean. Newer gas ranges, with electric pilot ignition, use no gas at all when the range is not in use and provide a cool appliance as well.

Gas-range burner holes should be entirely open. A stiff wire or an opened-up bobby pin is an easy tool to use to keep burner holes open. Yellow flame is usually a symptom of clogged holes. If cleaning them doesn't correct the condition, call your gas company for a service man to adjust the burners.

Your range should be level. If floor unevenness makes your range tilt even slightly in any direction, you'll bake cakes that are uneven because oven shelves are not level.

COOK AND SAVE

Cook on retained heat on your electric-range surface-cooking units. Simply turn off the switch and foods will finish cooking with no fuel cost at all. Units stay hot for quite a while after juice is turned off.

Cook with retained heat in either your gas or electric-range modern oven which is so well insulated you have to open the door to let the heat out if a recipe calls for starting high and finishing low-temperature baking or roasting. You can turn the modern range oven off a good half hour before end of cooking time and know your foods will be done to a turn.

Let your oven cook whole meals at once instead of a dish at a time. You'll save fuel costs, time and energy too.

Remove food for broiling from the refrigerator long enough ahead of cooking time so it's no longer chilled through. It will broil more quickly than if cooked directly from the refrigerator.

Pans staggered on your oven shelves, when baking, provide needed air circulation for best baking results and require the least comsumption of heat.

Save on gas. Keep a kettle of water over pilot light when gas range is not in use. Kettle keeps warm enough overnight for quick use in the morning. (This applies only to older ranges; new ones have electric ignition, no pilot lights any more.)

Why waste the bottom of your double boiler while cooking in the top? While you make a dessert or sauce in the top, your vegetables can cook simultaneously in the bottom of your double boiler.

Foods boil more quickly if pot covers fit snugly.

Select flat-bottom pans as wide in diameter or wider than cooking burners or heating elements. You simply waste heat around the edges of too-small pans.

Turn down the heat after foods begin to cook on top of the range. You'll cut fuel costs and foods will neither burn dry nor be shaken up and made unattractive because of too rapid boiling.

Add salt to the cooking water for vegetables in the bottom of your double boiler when the water's cold. Water will come to a boil faster.

Heat only as much water as you need, not a whole kettleful, for a cup of tea. In fact, there's a tiny teakettle that holds just enough water for a cup of tea or instant coffee, and a kettleful boils in only a few minutes.

Save fuel as well as vitamins and minerals by cooking vegetables in the smallest possible amount of boiling water for as short a time as possible. They look and taste better if still slightly crunchy when served, are more nutritious too. And short cooking conserves fuel.

Double-boiler food-saver. A jar lid placed in the double boiler will rattle when the water gets too low and thus give you a dependable SOS.

CLEANUP TIME

Don't let foods burn on. Wipe up food spills as fast as they occur and you'll preserve the porcelain-enamel finish of your range.

Stop frying-pan explosions. A little salt sprinkled in the frying pan will keep fat or lard from splattering. Also makes range cleaning easier.

When frying fish or meat, cover skillet with a colander. This allows steam to escape, permits food to brown well, and prevents grease from spattering.

Paper plates keep grease off burners and electric units. When frying food that tends to spatter grease, place paper plates over the burners or surface units not in use.

Surface units or burners should be kept clean. Electric units are, on the whole, self-cleaning, but you'll save yourself cleaning time if you line reflector pans with aluminum foil. Gas burners simply need to have holes kept free of burned-on foods, and burner holes should be kept open.

Set a pan of ammonia and water in your range oven overnight. In the morning cleaning the oven will be a breeze.

Foil broiler-pan cleaning with aluminum foil. Line the bottom part with foil to catch the drippings. Cover the top section with foil, too, and cut slits in it where the top part of the broiler pan is slit, to let juices escape to the bottom part.

If you have a corrugated, solid broiler pan, with a collecting trough at one end, shape your foil to fit that pan, with outside edges turned up.

Commercial oven cleaners, both solid and spray type, do a quick job. Be sure to follow container directions for use, however, and be safe by wearing rubber or other moisture-proof gloves.

It's easy to clean kitchen-range porcelain. Wait until it's cool, because porcelain enamel is glass-fused on steel and is breakable if misused. Use mild soap and warm water. Avoid cleaning powder and harsh abrasives which may scratch enamel finish.

Range enamel will last longer if you wait until cooking appliance cools before washing it, because water on warm enamel cools it more quickly than the base to which it is fused and may cause the enamel to crack.

Bacon drippings in oven? Turn off the pilot light, place a bowl of ammonia inside the oven, and close the door. The ammonia fumes will loosen the charred drippings and make the oven easy to clean.

In cleaning open-coil oven units, never put them into water. Wipe them off with a slightly damp cloth.

Broiler pan cleans easier the sooner you wash it after using. Don't leave uncleaned pan in oven, for stains will bake on and become difficult to remove.

REFRIGERATORS

Is your refrigerator door airtight? Models with magnetic closings and gaskets are practically permanent. But if yours is another model, make this simple test: Close the refrigerator door on a piece of paper. If the paper pulls out easily, chances are you are wasting gas or electricity and the door needs a new gasket.

Place your refrigerator on a cool kitchen wall. If it's next to a range or other heat-using appliance, the cold-food-storage appliance works overtime. Besides, it's ideal to have three work centers in your kitchen—refrigerator, range, and sink—as nearly in V formation as possible, so if you separate the refrigerator, as recommended, work will be easier in the room.

When off on vacation or even a week end, save gas or electricity by turning the cold control of your refrigerator down to the lowest operating point, just short of the defrost position on older refrigerator models.

Cool foods before you put them in your gas or electric refrigerator. It takes more power to cool hot foods in the refrigerator than it does if you let them come to room temperature first. If yours is a refrigerator that doesn't defrost automatically, you'll also have to defrost oftener because of excess moisture hot foods give off as they cool. With an automatic defroster, it will have to work overtime while hot foods cool.

Allow air space. Avoid crowding refrigerator shelves. To refrigerate properly, air must circulate inside the box.

Save that enamel. Acids corrode enamel. If vinegar,

lemon, or tomato spills in the refrigerator, wipe up immediately.

Deodorize inside of refrigerator by washing it with soapy water containing a little baking soda.

Another refrigerator deodorizer. A lump of charcoal in your refrigerator "sponges up" fish, onion, and other strong odors. Prevents them from penetrating butter, cheese, and other sensitive foods.

Ice cubes in a hurry. Store one or more large jars of water in your refrigerator. Use the water to refill ice trays. Since the water is already chilled, you'll have those extra ice cubes in jig-time when you want them for company.

Ice will freeze faster if you pour a little water on the surface where the tray sits. Be sure, however, not to have a heavy coating on the coils. Defrost well in advance of entertaining.

DEFROSTING

Use a reminder when defrosting if your refrigerator is one of the older models that must be defrosted. Are you one of those absent-minded people who forgets the refrigerator is being defrosted? Hang a sign on the handle with the word "defrosting" in large letters, to remind you to turn the knob back when the appliance is completely defrosted.

Modern refrigerators don't need to be defrosted. This is automatic these days. All you have to do to make the appliance give you full service is not to overcrowd the interior, clean it thoroughly every week or two, and give the exterior a regular application of a special wax designed for appliances with porcelain-enamel finish. Use if whether yours is white or one of the new colored appliances.

Quick defroster. When your refrigerator needs defrosting but frigid temperature is necessary to keep food from spoiling, try filling your ice-cube trays or pans with hot water. Repeat if necessary. The ice that coats the freezing unit will melt away in record time.

COOKING APPLIANCES

Microwave ovens are relatively new appliances that are still quite expensive to buy but that might prove economical over the long haul by cutting down on your utility bills. But most people will be interested in a microwave oven for its sheer convenience: it cooks foods extremely quickly and eliminates much of the mess of cleaning up. Despite the name, by the way, this appliance is not really a substitute for your oven, for many of the foods it cooks best—such as soups or frankfurters—are those usually cooked on range burners. Government and other tests have declared microwave ovens to be safe so long as the directions for use are followed, and they are not thought to have any side effects on people.

A portable oven makes a wonderful second oven if you have a range with one oven. It's a natural to fill and take along on picnics too, and for camp cookery where electricity is available.

Square or round? You have a wide choice of electric skillets these days. You might be used to non-electric round ones and prefer that shape. If you'd like to adventure a bit and have a little more cooking surface, there are square ones too. In any case, select one that has the plug at the end of the handle. These are easily washed right in the sink or dishpan.

Electric cookers, designed for deepfat frying and anything from making soup to stews and more exotic dishes, are fun for cooking at the table. To clean, you simply put water and dish-washing detergent or soap into the cooker, rinse with clear water, and wipe dry. Just be sure that you don't get water into the plug. Outside may be wiped with a damp cloth, polished with a dry one.

Crockpots are a special version of electric cookers designed to cook at low temperatures over long periods. Their main appeal is that you can prepare certain kinds of dishes and leave them to cook in the crockpot while you are away.

When you get a new toaster, check to be sure it is easy to clean. Nothing is more exasperating to a careful homemaker than a toaster with the problem of getting at stale crumbs in inaccessible corners.

To clean pop-up toaster, never, never shake it or poke into it with a harsh brush. Better use a chicken feather to brush out the crumbs. There's usually a hinged tray at the bottom, however, which you can unfasten by placing the toaster on its side. Swing it away from the toaster on its hinge, and it's easy to clean.

Toasters have gone big and glamorous. Look for them in decorator colors now. You might as well pick one that pretties your breakfast table as long as you're shopping for a new one. There's a huge one out now that takes two regular-width slices of bread in each slot; turn a knob and you can toast or broil in a tray at the bottom. The heating element turns on its side when you turn the knob.

Your gravy lumpy? Put it in your blender and in seconds it will be smooth as can be. The blender's wonderful, too, for smoothing applesauce, puréeing vegetables, and many other things you'll find in the recipe and instruction booklet that comes with it.

Electric-mixer blades are easy to clean if they come out easily and if they have no center shaft in the middle of the mixing end.

Here's how to clean your waffle iron: Scrub the grids with a fine wire brush, then brush them with non-salted oil. After this, heat the iron for about 10 minutes to recondition it. Soak up excess oil with a piece of bread placed between the grids.

Safest, most convenient can opener is the wall type. Get the detachable kind that can be removed from permanently mounted bracket for cleaning and storage (and can be folded back toward wall without detaching, when not in use). Among portable can openers, preferred type has circular cutting wheel.

Can openers need cleaning too. The cutting wheel gets gummy with food in time and should be cleaned very thoroughly. There's one can opener that comes with a spare wheel so the one that needs to be cleaned can go right into the dishpan.

You'll have keen knives if you keep an electric knife sharpener handy. A few strokes on each side of the knife and presto, it's sharp and safe to use again. Some sharpeners are even flexible enough so you can use them for sharpening scissors as well.

17

Kitchen Hints

TRICKS OF THE TRADE THAT SAVE TIME, WORK, AND MONEY

Spend a little more, save a lot. Buy best cooking equipment; better materials last longer, do a better job, give you tastier foods, cause less waste.

Kitchen tools need oiling? Apply a little glycerine with eye dropper. If any glycerine accidentally gets into food, don't worry. It's harmless.

Scales of household accuracy. Careful homemakers keep a kitchen scale handy. It's helpful in certain cookery and especially helpful in jam and jelly making. Handy for weighing Baby, too, with the aid of a well-padded large dishpan.

Measuring liquids is tricky. Undermeasuring is a common fault but can be avoided by setting measuring cup on level surface (otherwise the surface of liquid may slant and deceive you). Fill until liquid flows into correct groove mark of measuring cup.

Utensils darkened by heat absorb more heat than bright, shiny ones and often are responsible for over-browned or burned foods.

Brighten dulled aluminum pans by boiling some apple parings in them.

Aluminum dim-out. Don't worry if the bottoms of

your aluminum pans aren't too shiny. A dull surface absorbs more heat than a shiny one and cuts down fuel bills.

How to treat new skillets and pans. After greasing them well, place them in a 450° F. oven for about 30 minutes. Scour them well afterward, using fine steel wool, and wash in suds and water. Rinse and dry.

"Season" new enamelware by putting it in water and bringing to a boil slowly. Lengthens its life.

Look for these qualities in a carving set: Hardness of blade and sharpness of steel; initial sharpness of blade (to which it can be returned after it grows dull); resistance to stain and rust; resistance to warping; durability of handles.

Save kitchen knives from damage. Chop and cut foods on wooden cutting board. Protects other work surfaces, too, from being gouged by knife cuts.

Don't soak knives with painted handles. Soaking damages painted surfaces of any kind. In fact, any knife handle is liable to be undermined if soaked, since they are attached to the metal part by a variety of adhesives that don't take to soaking.

How to firm a food chopper. Place a piece of sandpaper under the clamp, with the rough side up, before tightening the screw to the table or pull-out shelf.

To keep whipping bowl from slipping, set it on a folded damp cloth.

For emergencies. A small coping saw of your own can be of great help when the butcher has not quite sawed the bone clear through. Also comes in handy when carving.

Pastry-brush longevity. It will last longer if you wash and dry it carefully after each use. Hang it up to dry where air circulates before putting it away.

New uses for old toothbrushes. Many thrifty homemakers have found them to be wonderfully handy for intricate cleaning chores. The bristles can penetrate into the hard-to-clean spots on numerous household gadgets, such as the gear-type can opener, egg beater, food chopper, grater, etc.

Salt flows freely, even in humid weather, if you keep a few grains of raw rice in the salt shaker.

CLEANUP TIME

Save dish-washing time. Use your china in rotation, so that there's never a group at the bottom of the pile that remains unused. Always take dishes from the bottom of the pile, and when they've been washed and wiped, return them to the top spot. That way none gathers dust.

Soak all cooking untensils if you haven't time to wash them up before dinner. They're much easier to wash later.

Don't rush hand dish-washing. If you use a good dish-washing detergent and plenty of hot water, you'll find dish-washing much easier if you let them soak in the water and detergent for a half hour before proceeding with the job.

The cool treatment. Always let metal cake pans cool before washing, to prevent warping of the metal.

When pot and kettle call each other black. To clean the inside of pot or kettle, slice a lemon and put the slices in an aluminum coffeepot with plenty of cold water. Let it come to a boil and keep it boiling until the inside surface can be made to look like new just by rubbing the surface with a cloth.

How to rescue a burned or greasy pan. Fill the pan with an inch of water, add 1 tablespoonful or more of soda, and heat the water to the boiling point.

Clean greasy frying pans with ease. Put a small amount of soap powder in the pan, add warm water, and simmer slowly for a few minutes. In this way even the greasiest of frying pans can be cleaned in a matter of seconds.

To "de-fish" or "de-onionize" utensils, put a few drops of ammonia in the dish water when washing used dishes. Or put several tablespoons of vinegar in the dish water; fish and onion odors disappear just like that. Another quick deodorizer consists of washing, scalding, then inverting the utensils over a gas flame for about 2 minutes.

Remove teakettle coating. When lime settles on the inside of your teakettle, don't wait until the coating gets thick. Make it a point to use the teakettle every time you want to boil potatoes or boil the peelings from carrots. Either one keeps the inside of your tea-kettle free of lime coating.

Save lemon skin after squeezing juice. Use rind to remove mineral stains from insides of teapots and other vessels. Fill utensil with lukewarm water. Add cut-up skin of 1 lemon (with pulp still attached) for each pint of water. Allow it to soak for 4 or 5 hours. Rinse kettle with hot water.

Never scour Pyrex cooking utensils with steel wool or scrape them with a knife. In doing so, you may scratch the surface of the glass. Wash glass utensils by soaking them in lukewarm suds, rinsing with lukewarm water. If brown stains appear on the glass, rub them with dry baking soda before washing or use a mild scouring powder on them.

To clean the inside of a Pyrex teakettle, half fill it with water, add a few small pieces of lemon. Let water boil, then pour off; finally, rinse in fresh water.

Removing remains of burned food from an enamel-ware pot. Soak pot overnight with water and washing or baking soda. Wash it the next morning in soapsuds, then rinse carefully with clear water. Don't use a knife to scrape off burned particles if you don't want the enamel to chip; it's glass, you know.

Never soak an earthenware dish or pot if food has scorched in it. Add a teaspoonful of baking soda to the water and let it stand only until particles have loosened.

Crusted casseroles. When burned food is hard to clean from casseroles, fill them with warm water and add a teaspoonful of baking soda. The crusted matter will loosen quickly.

Clean out hard-to-remove sediment that often clings to bottom of bottle or glass vase by filling vessel half full with warm soapsuds, then add a handful of carpet tacks. Shake vigorously and watch the sediment loosen.

After grinding other foods (meats, nuts, etc.), grind through a piece of dried bread. This carries sticky food particles away and makes grinder washing easy.

Toothbrush cleans egg beater. Gets into spots that are difficult to penetrate otherwise. Also handy when cleaning food choppers, graters, etc. (Jewelry too.)

Egg beaters and potato mashers wash easily and quickly if you place them in cold water as soon as you've used them.

Rust remover. Dip rusted metalware in pure cider vinegar, then let it dry for a few days. Wipe away the remaining loosened rust particles.

Rust rings caused by scouring-powder cans sitting on shelves in the bathroom or kitchen can be prevented by covering the bottom edges of the can with strips of Scotch tape.

Keep faucets shiny bright. Rub the brass or other metal with furniture polish after cleaning.

Don't clog your drain with grease. When pouring off fats, lay a few pieces of newspaper over the drain before you pour. The grease will then remain on the paper, while the water will naturally disappear, thus saving you clogged drainpipes and nasty plumbing jobs.

KITCHEN COMFORT

Good-by to unwelcome cooking odors. Neutralize them by boiling 3 teaspoonfuls ground clove in 2 cups water for 15 minutes. Or heat some vinegar on the range. Works like a charm.

Banish workaday odors from your hands. Remove clinging odor of onions, fish, or oil from hands and dishes by rubbing with moistened salt. Rinse well with clear water, then wash with soap. Or just rinse with vinegar.

Sinks smell better. A handful of baking soda put in the sink overnight will clean and purify that unfragrant drain.

Less noise in the kitchen. Cover work counters or shelves with sound-deadening linoleum, vinyl, Formica, or tile. They are also easily kept clean by wiping with damp cloth.

You can replace existing sink faucets with dishwashing equipment. It works like a faucet, too. There's a brush at the end of a hose, a detergent well behind the faucet part. When you turn on the water it comes through the brush. Press a button and the water and detergent mix. You can thus wash with much hotter water than your hands can stand in the dishpan.

You'll cook in cool comfort if you have an air conditioner in your kitchen as well as a ventilating fan. Your appliance dealer will tell you the best location for each of these luxuries so they'll perform at peak perfection and most economical operating cost.

Save your larger-size paper grocery bags. They make excellent linings for garbage pail or wastebasket, make disposal of refuse easier, keep receptacle clean. Paper-bag-line all your wastebaskets, for the same reasons.

LITTLE THINGS MAKE A BIG DIFFERENCE

Save screw-top glass containers from coffee, jams, etc., and you'll save money. Use them for storing dry foods such as cereals, flour, and dried vegetables. These foods, if kept in original cardboard containers during warm months, tend to foster growth of bacteria. Not so in airtight covered glass jars.

With glass containers for foods in the pantry, you can always tell when you are running low on an item and can replenish the supply before you're out of stock.

Fasten linoleum to kitchen shelves with linoleum cement and it will practically never come off. It will also look handsome and clean easily with a damp cloth.

Solids won't go through your funnel? Keep a knitting needle handy, the plastic kind that won't rust. It's perfect to use as a plunger in the narrow funnel opening.

Use your sieve or colander when changing flower water. You'll catch the bits of leaves and other deposit in the water that might in time clog up your drain.

Saucy sieve successes. Sauce lumpy? Simply force it through a sieve, using a wooden spoon or rubber scraper to speed the process. Works as well with gravy too.

Paper toweling makes an excellent "blotter" for draining foods that are fried in deep fat.

Candlelight can be beautiful, unless the romantic touches start to drip. Avoid messy candles by putting them in refrigerator for a few hours before using.

Heatproof table mats can be made by mounting colorful lengths of linoleum on pieces of plywood. Cement linoleum to the plywood, then paint edges a bright color.

Morning time-saver for busy bodies. Set your table for breakfast the night before and save precious time in the morning when every minute counts.

Good breakfasts can be made quickly. If dry ingredients for muffins or pancakes are mixed the night before (and muffin tins greased), many precious minutes can be saved during the breakfast rush.

Toast for invalids. Just before serving eggs on toast to invalids (and children), cut the toast into cubes, leaving the slice in its original shape before putting the egg over it. Easier to handle, and coaxes feeble appetites.

When a convalescent child loses interest in food, try this: paste attractive cutouts to outside bottom of drinking glass, glass bowl, or glass dish. Use any good mending adhesive for pasting on the cutouts. You thus make a game of mealtime and give ailing child a new incentive for "cleaning the plate."

18

Measures and Weights

REVIEW FAMILIAR MEASURES AND GET A HEAD START ON THINKING METRIC IN THE KITCHEN

What is the metric system? It's a simple way of measuring that is based on the decimal system, with units increasing or decreasing in size by 10s.

How would a change to the metric system affect your cooking habits? Very little to begin with, because a conversion to the system will take many years. But since nearly every country in the world is "thinking metric," it is well to have an idea of what the system is all about. To give you that idea we suggest a look at the following section on Measures and Weights. In its pages you will find Standard U. S. Measures and Weights with Equivalents in other units of the same system; Metric Measures and Weights with Equivalents in other units of the same system; Metric Equivalents of U. S. Measures and Weights, and U. S. Equivalents of Metric Measures and Weights; Conversion Tables showing you how to convert common kitchen units from the U.S. system to the metric system and from the metric system to the U.S. system.

As an extra kitchen helper we have provided a Temperature Conversion Table that enables you to convert

Fahrenheit and Celsius temperatures from one to the other plus a list of most commonly used oven temperatures in both the Fahrenheit and Celsius scales.

LIQUID MEASURE

UNIT	ABBR.	EQUIVALENTS IN OTHER UNITS OF SAME SYSTEM
gill	gi.	¼ pint (4 fluid ounces)
pint	pt.	4 gills (16 fluid ounces)
quart	qt.	2 pints (32 fluid ounces)
gallon	gal.	4 quarts (128 fluid ounces)
½ cup		gill (4 fluid ounces)
cup		½ pint (8 fluid ounces)
2 cups		pint (16 fluid ounces)
4 cups		quart (32 fluid ounces)

DRY MEASURE

pint	pt.	½ quart
quart	qt.	2 pints
peck	pk.	8 quarts
bushel	bu.	4 pecks

AVOIRDUPOIS WEIGHT

grain	gr.	0.036 dram
dram	dr.	27.34 grains
ounce	oz.	437.5 grains or 16 drams
pound	lb.	7,000 grains or 16 ounces

LIQUID AND DRY MEASURES*

teaspoon	tsp.	⅓ tablespoon
tablespoon	tbs.	3 teaspoons
¼ cup		4 tablespoons
⅓ cup		5 tablespoons + 1 teaspoon
½ cup		8 tablespoons
⅔ cup		10 tablespoons + 2 teaspoons
¾ cup		12 tablespoons
cup		16 tablespoons

METRIC SYSTEM

CAPACITY

UNIT	ABBR.	EQUIVALENTS IN OTHER UNITS OF THE SAME SYSTEM
milliliter	ml	0.001 liter
centiliter	cl	0.01 liter
deciliter	dl	0.1 liter
liter	l	10 deciliters or 100 centiliters or 1,000 milliliters
decaliter	dkl	10 liters
hectoliter	hl	100 liters

WEIGHT OR MASS

milligram	mg	0.001 gram
centigram	cg	0.01 gram
decigram	dg	0.1 gram
gram	g	10 decigrams or 100 centigrams or 1,000 milligrams
decagram	dkg	10 grams
hectogram	hg	100 grams
kilogram	kg	1,000 grams

* All measures are level

U. S. SYSTEM WITH METRIC EQUIVALENTS

LIQUID MEASURE

U.S. UNIT	METRIC EQUIVALENT
gill	0.118 liter
pint	0.473 liter
quart	0.946 liter
gallon	3.785 liters

DRY MEASURE

pint	0.551 liter
quart	1.101 liters
peck	8.810 liters
bushel	35.239 liters

AVOIRDUPOIS WEIGHT

ounce	28.349 grams
pound	453.59 grams

LIQUID AND DRY MEASURES

teaspoon	5 milliliters
tablespoon	15 milliliters
¼ cup	60 milliliters
⅓ cup	80 milliliters
½ cup	120 milliliters
⅔ cup	160 milliliters
¾ cup	180 milliliters
cup	240 milliliters
	or 0.24 liter

METRIC SYSTEM WITH U. S. EQUIVALENTS

CAPACITY

METRIC UNIT	U.S. UNIT (LIQUID)	U.S. UNIT (DRY)
milliliter	0.034 fluid ounce	
centiliter	0.338 fluid ounce	

METRIC UNIT	U.S. UNIT (LIQUID)	U.S. UNIT (DRY)
deciliter	0.21 pint	0.18 pint
liter	1.05 quarts	0.908 quart
decaliter	2.64 gallons	1.14 pecks
hectoliter	26.418 gallons	2.84 bushels

WEIGHT OR MASS

METRIC UNIT	U.S. UNIT
milligram	0.0154 grain
centigram	0.1543 grain
decigram	1.543 grain
gram	15.43 grains or 0.03527 ounce
decagram	0.3527 ounce
hectogram	3.527 ounces
kilogram	2.2046 pounds

CONVERSION TABLES

The tables below are set up to help you convert the most common kitchen units from one system of Measures and Weights to the other. The answers you arrive at will be approximate but near enough to absolute accuracy for nonscientific pursuits.

WHEN YOU KNOW the U.S. unit	MULTIPLY BY:	TO FIND the metric unit
Teaspoons	5	Milliliters
Tablespoons	15	Milliliters
Fluid Ounces	30	Milliliters
Fluid Ounces	0.03	Liters
Cups	240	Milliliters
Cups	0.24	Liters
Pints	0.47	Liters
Quarts	0.95	Liters
Gallons	3.8	Liters
Ounces	28	Grams
Pounds	454	Grams
Pounds	0.45	Kilograms

WHEN YOU KNOW the metric unit	MULTIPLY BY:	TO FIND the U.S. unit
Milliliters	0.2	Teaspoons
Milliliters	0.07	Tablespoons
Milliliters	0.034	Fluid Ounces
Liters	34	Fluid Ounces
Milliliters	0.004	Cups
Liters	4.2	Cups
Liters	2.1	Pints
Liters	1.06	Quarts
Liters	0.26	Gallons
Grams	0.035	Ounces
Grams	0.002	Pounds
Kilograms	2.2	Pounds

CONVERTING TEMPERATURES

To convert from Fahrenheit to Celsius, subtract 32 from the Fahrenheit reading, multiply the figure left by 5, and divide the product by 9.
Example: $65° F—32=33$; $33×5=165$; $165÷9=18.3°C$.
To convert from Celsius to Fahrenheit, multiply the Celsius reading by 9, divide the product by 5, and add 32. *Example:* $35° C.×9=315$; $315÷5=63$; $63+32=95° F$.
On the Fahrenheit scale, water boils at about 212° and freezes at about 32°. On the Celsius scale, water boils at about 100° and freezes at about 0°.

THE MOST COMMONLY USED OVEN TEMPERATURES

OVEN TEMPERATURES	FAHRENHEIT SCALE	CELSIUS SCALE
Very slow	Below 300°	Below 149.0°
Slow	300°	149.0°

OVEN TEMPERATURES	FAHRENHEIT SCALE	CELSIUS SCALE
Moderately slow	325°	162.8°
Moderate	350°	176.7°
Moderately hot	375°	190.6°
Hot	400–425°	204.4–218.3°
Very hot	450–475°	232.2–246.1°
Extremely hot	500° or more	260.0° or more

19

Personal Appearance

A NATURAL APPROACH TO CULTIVATING GOOD LOOKS ALSO CONNECTS WITH HEALTH AND HAPPINESS

Don't neglect the importance of frequent and regular exercise to the health, well-being, and personal appearance of all the members of the family. Exercise and fresh air improve the circulation and muscle tone, keep figures trim, increase over-all vitality. Tennis, golf, bicycling, hiking, running, badminton, and volleyball are all healthful recreational activities that the whole family can enjoy together, often at moderate cost. Find out if there's a YM-YWCA or community center near your home that offers a program of sports and recreational activities, and apply for a family membership.

Good posture hides waistline bulges. When working, cleaning, or walking, remember to stretch to your full height and keep your shoulders back, tummy in, rear under. Cultivate the good-posture habit and you'll soon be walking in beauty, go much longer before you tire.

Lift your chin off your chest, unfold your neck, and look up for beauty's sake. When you read, walk, write, think, drive your car, or talk, lift up your chin, hold up your head, and unfold the creases of your neck. By doing this you will not only augment the beauty of your neck but you'll add grace to everything you do.

Are you one of those who should eat more? Does it take you twice as long to get rested? Half as long to get tired? Do you feel and look as though you'd lost your luster? Are you a pushover for the first fall sniffles? It may well be that you don't eat enough. Watch your calories if you must watch your weight, but make up for it in vitamins, proteins, and don't go around hungry. Vitality is the most important beauty factor you have.

You have to work on the art of relaxation. Don't think you're relaxing just because you tie on a dressing gown and stretch out full length on a couch. You have to "work at it." Here are two relaxing exercises and seven other energy-saving tips:

1. S-t-r-e-t-c-h-i-n-g: Catch the footboard of your bed with your toes and grasp the headboard with both hands. Pull toward the headboard, sliding your body upward, until your head almost touches it. Repeat until tensions go and a sensation of release spreads over you.

2. Shake like a puppy. Stand up, bend over, let arms hang limply and shake.

When you feel low, it's not easy to be bright and gay every single day of the week. We are all subjected to moods of depression and an occasional "blue Monday." Don't make the mistake, however, of matching your mood with drab costume colors. Instead bring out the gayest and brightest of all your costumes and deliberately set about to squelch that mood.

LITTLE THINGS COUNT

Never overlook any detail, from head to toe, that might spoil your appearance. No woman can be truly glamorous—even though her hair and make-up have a look of perfection and her dress is a compliment to her taste—if her shoes are not attractive. Hands that aren't clean and carefully manicured also will cancel an otherwise glamorous impression. By paying attention to these small details you can consistently look your best.

To be serene, and to "feel" well groomed is as important a beauty asset as physical good looks. Avoid clothes and cosmetics that make you do constant checking while you wear them.

Wear a stole that can be anchored, one that fastens with a self-fabric loop or buckle.

If you wear nearly backless shoes, see that they have magnetic soles that grip your feet. Backless shoes that wobble, slip off, or slap up and down not only make the wearer nervous, but also every man who watches helplessly while she clatters by.

Keep the disheveling wind out of your coiffure either by wearing a tie-on veil or spraying on a coating of lacquer that can be brushed out when you get to your destination.

If you wear a shallow hat, keep it in place by sewing to the sweatband small grip-tooth combs to catch your hair, or tie your hat on with a veil.

Sew tiny inside holders to shoulder line of garments so there's not a constant struggle with straps of bras and slips.

If you wear a strapless gown, use double-face adhesive strip to keep it from slipping. Tugging up a gown can become almost as unattractive a public habit as pulling down your girdle or foundation garment.

FACE THE FACTS

Pick her carefully. Many women, especially the younger set of beauty seekers, secretly select some current beauty of the stage or screen or TV after whom to pattern their beauty scheme. Too often, however, they select an inappropriate model for their own particular kind of beauty, and the results are unnatural and far from lovely.

Find your double. Remember that there are different kinds of blondes, brunettes, brownettes, and redheads, so be sure to find the one who resembles you in many ways.

Never forget that you are you. Use these lovely women of the stage and screen as models from whom to get ideas for your make-up, your coiffure, your fashions, etc., only because they are groomed by experts in the grooming arts and not because you wish to look and act exactly like them. Then adapt the ideas you gather so that they may enhance your own individual personality and make you a more beautiful, well-groomed "you."

Suppose you have a plumpish face and neck that you'd like to lengthen a bit? Bedeck yourself as dazzlingly as Marco Polo in a long necklace of eye-pulling color. Pin it into a V at the neckline with a jewel. That device can be as effective as a lighted road sign in flagging eyes to a longer route.

For another way to achieve a longish effect, wear graduated ropes of beads. Don't have the first rope start too high. Let ropes fall on an open neck or spill their splendor over a dress, shirt or sweater.

If you face is long and your neck a bit angular, the choker or dog collar has a foreshortening effect. A bib of beads is just as effective. Besides reducing apparent length of the neck, the graduated ropes of beads will hide angular neckbones.

Your teeth are important. Your teeth may not be perfect and even, but your mouth can still be attractive if your teeth are sparkling. Regular dental care is the best assurance for keeping teeth in good condition. The most carefully applied lipstick won't hide neglected teeth. When you speak or smile your teeth become a focal point and they can spoil an otherwise beautifully groomed appearance or be the "extra plus" that makes you truly attractive.

Clear-eyed beauty. The best eye care is, of course, lots of sleep and avoidance of overstraining through reading, sewing, movies, or TV. If your eyes get tired easily, bathe occasionally with soothing eye lotion and check with your eye doctor as to whether you need glasses.

"Can't do a thing with your hair?" Try adding this simple ritual to your daily beauty program: Bend over and brush your scalp and hair from back to front until your scalp tingles. Then massage scalp with fingertips and see how easy to manage your hair becomes.

SKIN CARE

How to outwit your skin's worst foe, dry indoor heat. Considering the drying effects of steam and dry heat on skins that are naturally dry, it's no wonder that so many women and girls lack the lovely freshness of face that is their birthright, for the drying effects are forerunners of premature lines and wrinkles. Here are some combat tactics to defeat this enemy:

Lower the thermostat to 68° F., or under. If you don't believe your skin suffers in an overheated room, watch an ivy plant (the hardiest) wither in a higher temperature.

Place a humidifier, or an ordinary basin of water, in any heated room.

Go easy on soap and water for a couple of months while the heater in the basement is being stoked. Substitute cleansing creams which won't further deplete your skin of natural oils.

Be faithful in use of night cream. See that this oil replenisher is rich in oils.

Don't cancel out the good work your night cream does by wearing a make-up the next day that draws natural moisture from your skin like a dry sponge.

Wear instead a creamy type of foundation make-up. There's rejuvenating moisture, all-day protection, and actually a beauty treatment in creamy make-up foundations.

Before you apply one single beauty requisite to your face always make sure it is thoroughly cleansed with your cleansing cream. Use your fingertips or a natural-silk sponge to spread the cream over your entire face. Then allow it to remain on your face long enough to clease all dirt and grime from the pores. Removing the cleansing cream from your face is equally as important as its application. So wipe away all traces of the cream, using a soft clean towel or a facial tissue. Complete the cleansing process with an application of a skin freshener or astringent. And for a cooling pickup on hot days, keep your skin freshener or astringent in the refrigerator.

Regular skin care is essential even for the youngest girl. Your daily skin cleansing should become a night and morning habit. Each night remove your make-up with cleansing cream and wash your face thoroughly with a mild soap and warm water. Then follow with an application of skin freshener or astringent. Even though your skin is oily, it needs lubrication, but not as frequently as a dry skin. Use your sleeping hours for this lubrication by applying a night cream before retiring. In the morning your skin care ritual can be a very simple face washing followed by an application of skin freshener or astringent. Then you are ready for your make-up.

BEWARE OF BEAUTY THIEVES!

The most common, most wanton thief of beauty is the blackhead that makes its appearance on the sides of the face where it often cannot be seen when looking into a mirror front view. It first appears as a pinpoint blackhead of no great consequence, and because it cannot be easily seen, it grows until it is big, black, and the size of the head of a pin. Often such blackheads appear just inside of the ears, on the lobes of ears, or along the hairline. They should be removed before they gain large proportions. If, however, in your search you find that such a thief has invaded your beauty territory and has grown to a larger size than you believe it is wise to handle, let your doctor or dermatologist remove it for you, so that a scar may not take its place.

If blackheads have become so large that infection has started, if they are stubborn and will not come out with gentle pressure, or if certain areas of the skin are filled with many blackheads, visit your dermatologist before trouble begins. Never try to remove such blackheads yourself, for your skin is precious, and the lack of professional care and advice may mean the difference between a perfect skin and a scarred one.

After your blackheads are gone, follow a thorough day-by-day cleansing routine, so that your pretty face will be as free and smooth, when school reopens this fall, as the palm of your hand.

Another glamour thief is the wild hair or hairs that often grow out of the chin, nose, or at the sides of the face where they are not too obvious at first glance. Once seen, however, they become an obsession with the observer. Keep these plucked out with tweezers, being sure to apply alcohol or astringent before and after the plucking. Hairs that grow out of the nose, and gain such length that they can be seen, should be snipped with fingernail scissors, not plucked. If hairs are growing out of a mole, consult your doctor before touching them. He will know how you should remove them so they will not rob you of your beauty.

Avoid a red nose from head colds or wintry winds. Best concealment of a leaky nose's unwanted redness is to use a make-up from a neat, compact cake which you can carry with you. For those inevitable repairs, you'll need to carry your make-up and reapply it often.

Camouflage for blemishes. Skin blemishes can be retouched on you much as the negatives of photographs can be retouched to give a flawless print. The way to do it is with products especially made for this purpose: cream-stick "eraser," or a heavy, dry "coverall" cream. Either should be of the kind that vanishes into the skin while covering up the blemished spot. Slight blending may be necessary. The camouflaging should be applied in a skin-matching or foundation-matching shade to soft-focus any flaws or imperfections in your complexion, whether temporary or permanent. Choose a cover-aid that is smooth and soft, but not greasy. Use it under your make-up, but over a cream foundation, covering it all with powder. Beware of applying the "camouflage" heavily, or it will cake and call attention to the imperfection instead of hiding it.

To minimize a vaccination scar, and other spots that seem to grow whiter the darker your skin tans, use a pastel cream rouge over these body marks. Rouge brings up the red pigment that's been lost, blends scar tissue to a pale pink. But practice to get the exact amount of rouge over the scar, since this is the trick of canceling out whiteness. Now apply a cake make-up of a shade that matches your tan and blend around scar. If patchwork is still not perfect, dust some of your tan face powder over the mark in a still wider area.

EIGHT SUMMER PICK-ME-UPS

A generous dousing of your body with your favorite cologne (first cooled in your refrigerator for this purpose) feels wonderful on a hot summer day. Especially dab some on your wrists and the soles of your feet. . . . Is that you purring?

Take hot baths, for if you bathe in water that is warmer than the air, you feel cooler when you get out of the bath. Use cologne after the bath, talcum on the soles of your feet to lessen friction between feet and shoes.

Wear cotton eyelet and other self-ventilating fabrics, as cooling as air conditioning in hot weather.

Set your hair with a little cologne. It's cooling and refreshing to your scalp, helps hair waft a heavenly fragrance.

Before repowdering your face, press over it a face towel wrung out in cold, even icy water.

Keep feet cool and comfortable by changing hosiery during the day, even more than once if you happen to stroll by the stocking box.

Keep colognes, skin fresheners, astringent, cotton pads for cooling eyelids in the refrigerator.

Eat summer's lighter-caloried foods: Vegetables and fruits. See that you have sufficient salt in your diet. Drink lots of water and cooling beverages.

TRICKS FOR SPEEDING UP
A SUN TAN

In a hurry to look like a gypsy? You'll tan faster if you strike out for the sun's gold in white clothes. White all down the line, from towels to sun hat, will reflect sun rays, enable you to get an even, quicker, more spectacular tan.

Don't wash off that vitamin D. If you dash into a shower bath too soon after your sun bath, you'll risk washing off valuable vitamin D before your skin has had enough time to absorb all of it.

How to repel seepage into your swim cap. If you've tried simply everything to keep your curls dry under a swim cap, maybe you've overlooked the one trick that champion divers use: a chamois band, 4 to 5 inches wide, wound around your head. Hair is pushed over band, the chamois is folded once, wrapped snugly, and fastened with a hook and eye or by tying the string attached to each end.

BEAUTY FROM YOUR KITCHEN

Fruits, vegetables, and dairy products are not only good for you to eat—they can also do wonders for your skin and hair when applied externally. Your refrigerator and pantry contain the ingredients for homemade beauty preparations as effective as expensive commercial cosmetics—and you can eat the leftovers! Here are some natural beauty recipes you might like to try:

Farm-fresh skin care. Dry, reddened skin can be soothed by an application of the "milk" from scraped corn kernels. If skin is oily, rub a cut slice of tomato on it, allow the juice to dry, then rinse with cool water.

Another good astringent for oily skin is parsley tea. Steep a handful of parsley in boiling water for a few minutes, allow to cool to room temperature, and splash on face and neck.

A paste of steamed and puréed carrots is beneficial against acne and other skin inflammations. Spread the paste on inflamed areas, leave on for 30 minutes, then rinse with cool water.

Give yourself a delightful pore-opening facial by steeping fresh mint leaves in boiling water in a large shallow enamel pan. Drape a bath towel over your head, bend over the pan, and let your face bask in the fragrant steam.

A cucumber mask gently cleanses the skin and, if used regularly, lightens and evens out skin tones. Grind up a large, unpeeled cucumber in the blender and strain the juice through a triple thickness of cheesecloth. Mix the juice with the whites of two eggs until smooth, then add 2 tablespoons of 90 proof vodka and one tablespoon lemon juice. For extra astringency, ¼ teaspoon of peppermint extract may be added.

Here's a recipe for a delectable, moisturizing avocado-honey mask: In a blender or electric beater, combine 1 tablespoon mashed avocado, 2 tablespoons raw honey, and 2 egg whites or 1 whole egg. Blend at high speed and smooth over your face.

Home treatment for dandruff. Apply hot olive oil several hours before shampooing. Shampoo scalp thoroughly with tincture of green soap, which you can buy at any drugstore.

A well-beaten egg blended with 1 cup of your favorite shampoo will give your hair extra shine and body.

Rinsing your hair regularly with sage tea after shampooing helps curb dandruff and is also said to darken gray hairs.

Lemon juice makes a safe, inexpensive and easy-to-apply bleach, if your hair is already light. A mild preparation may be made with a cup of 15 per cent alcohol, the juice of a lemon, and a drop or two of glycerine.

A natural body rub for soothing sore muscles may be made as follows: In an enamel saucepan, heat ¼ cup lanolin, ¼ cup sesame or safflower oil, and 3 tablespoons oil of wintergreen. Stir well and remove from heat. When cool, add ½ cup water and mix with electric mixer on high speed.

Mix your own delicious toothpaste by combining 2 tablespoons baking soda with 2 tablespoons powdered cinnamon and 2 tablespoons oil of cinnamon.

20

Your Wardrobe

HOW TO CARE FOR YOUR CLOTHES AND SHOES TO REMAIN WELL DRESSED ON A·BUDGET

Save garment with clever embroidery trick. Cover a small hole in a blouse or dress with a pretty bit of colorful embroidery design, and actually profit by an accident to the fabric by giving the garment a new look. Cover frayed cuffs with a closely sewn blanket stitch and add matching touch at neckline.

Chain stitch has many uses as wardrobe-saver. Makes new button loops for those small under-the-collar buttons on coats, dresses, blouses. It's handy for inconspicuous belt loops, makes firm anchor between the coat lining and the outer fabric, allows the lining to hang freely so it doesn't bulge at the hemline.

Don't let yourself be embarrassed by a loose hem. Use the catch stitch to make it secure. Work from left to right on the wrong side of the dress or skirt, catching several threads of material above the seam tape. Pull thread through gently.

Have you a growing daughter? Let out the hems of her dresses at the end of the season, before they're cleaned or laundered and stored. When she's ready to wear them again and needs dresses a little longer, a new hem can be made without any telltale mark to show the position of last year's line.

When that ugly hemline shows, the nap or finish usually has worn off so that the line cannot be removed. Just cover the telltale mark with a narrow ribbon or braid resembling the present trimming. Or make a tuck with the old hemline concealed on the underside. The result is often prettier, smarter than before.

Save your coat from puckering. If it is sewed together at the hem, separate the lining and outer material. One or the other fabric may shrink; ugly, cheap-looking puckers and bulges are then caused by the shrinkage. For a smart, trim look, re-hem both outer material and lining and let them hang free at the hemline.

Friction foiler. Elbows of long-sleeved woolen dresses usually are the first to show wear. Reinforce these weak spots by sewing an oblong piece of light-weight fabric of the same color inside the elbow.

Line the pockets of trousers with chamois to protect them from tears made by nails, bolts, and small tools carried around by some men.

Protect rough-and-tumble knees of children and pants with knee patches that iron on. They're marvelous on playsuits, corduroys, overalls, blue jeans, work slacks, snow suits, ski suits, etc. Get the kind that will wash and dry-clean with garment.

ZIPPER SURGERY

To remesh a zipper that pulls out of the slider, remove the slider to the open end, hold it loosely, and insert end tooth on the pull-out side into the slider where it belongs. Be careful to hold flat the rest of the zipper in front of the slider, so that the two sides are exactly parallel and so close they almost touch. If you are holding them correctly, you can hold the ends of the tape as the slider pulls up and meshes the teeth.

When a zipper jams. You'll probably find that paper or thread particles are interfering with its free play. These must be removed patiently. Wherever an end of thread or fabric protrudes, pull it out gently. If the slider still jams, move it back and forth until you loosen the impediment. Always hold the slider by the tab. Never push, pull, or poke.

Zippers always work smoothly when teeth are rubbed occasionally with a bit of wax.

HOW TO COPE WITH SHINE, LINT, HAIRLINES

Remove shine from wool clothes. Sponge garment with solution of 1 teaspoon ammonia to a quart of water. Press on wrong side.

Another shine remover. Rub with a pressing cloth moistened with a mild vinegar solution, to raise the nap, then again moisten the cloth and use it as a regular ironing cloth for pressing.

Remove shine from serge, as well as worsted gabardines, flannels, and worsted wools in general, by dampening a sponge or cloth slightly and sponging the shiny parts quite thoroughly. While fabric is still damp, go over it, gently, with fine steel wool. Stroke the fabric with this, covering about 6 inches of the suit with each stroke. Results will amaze you, usually giving plenty of new life to an old suit. (Do not try this on cottons or rayons.)

Hairlines are danger lines on men's and women's clothes. Once that oil mark hardens in the fabric, it may prove impossible to remove completely. So, once weekly, clean coat-collar hairlines with a cleanser containing a grease solvent and brush briskly afterward.

Vacuum-clean clothes. Loose dust and dirt won't harden and cut men's and boys' suits if you take advantage of the small, stiff brush attachment that comes with most vacuum cleaners. (Be sure the brush itself is clean before using it on clothing.) Notice how it sucks out the dirt and, in tweeds and heavy woolens, revives the texture.

GETTING THE HANG OF IT

The wrong way is right. Put garments on hangers wrong side out. Keeps them clean longer.

Here's a trick up your nonexistent sleeve. To prevent sleeveless garments from slipping off wire hangers, bend up both ends of the hanger.

Anti-wrinkle tip. While it still retains body heat, put right on a hanger the suit or dress you've just taken off. The wrinkles will fall out more easily.

Prevent a trouser crease where it doesn't belong. To avoid a horizontal midway crease, put a newspaper over the hanger rod, then fold trousers over the paper.

Wire hangers won't rust-stain clothes if you wind cellulose tape around them.

Do wire hangers cave in under weight of heavy garments? Double their strength by binding two hangers together with cellulose or adhesive tape.

To prevent wooden garment hangers from snagging fabric give them a coat of clear shellac. Allow to dry well. Wood won't chip or sliver if protected this way.

STORAGE TIPS

Number the shirts. Shirts should be rotated so that each gets equal wear. Why not number each shirt inside the neckband, to help keep track?

Fade-out on fading. Clothes of aquamarine and some shades of blue, purple, and gray tend to fade. They'll stay their true color longer if you store them between wearings in a black cloth bag or in black wrapping paper.

To protect delicate lace articles, keep them beautiful and durable, wrap them in waxed paper. Prevents threads from rotting.

ENEMY NUMBER 1 FOR CLOTHES: PERSPIRATION

Prevent underarm "mystery holes." Most deodorants are chemicals that may be gentle on the skin but, when freshly applied, may eat into the fabrics they touch. Remedy: when deodorant dries, dust underarm with talcum powder.

Dress color vs. perspiration. Don't let perspiration ruin those beautiful dress colors or weaken the fabric. Large-size dress shields give real protection, in addition to regular use of an underarm deodorant.

Remove arm shields before cleaning, because, if of doubtful quality, steam may soften and smear the rubberized fabric.

Perspiration can ruin coats, too. Tack lining-cloth shields in armholes of coats to protect against perspiration and wear.

Angora sweaters, gloves, and scarves are beautiful, but how they shed! Unless you're in on this little secret: keep angoras in your refrigerator between wearings. Works wonders.

Fur protection. Fur will last lots longer, look much better, if the closet in which you keep it is humidified. Place inside the closet a bowl of water into which you've put a sponge. Renew the water before it evaporates.

Give extra protection, not only from moths but also from dust, to babies' little knit bonnets, winter leggings, jackets, angora mittens, sweaters, woolen hats and caps; to Argyle socks, ski suits. Make sure they're all clean, then wrap in a package of aluminum foil, also including a sprinkling of paradichloride crystals. If the garment is large, join several lengthwise pieces of the foil together, double-folding along the lengthwise edge so it is wide enough to take such things as ski clothes. Use a double fold in joining outer edges together also, forming an envelope that is airtight. This way garments really have absolute protection.

HOW TO STARVE MOTHS

Your mothproofing money's worth. Moth preventatives should be hung as high as possible in the clothes closet, because the fumes filter downward. Otherwise you get only partial protection.

Moths love woolens. Woolens don't love moths. One sure way to keep them apart in summertime is to store unused sweaters and other woolens in large jars stuffed with moth balls, the lid turned down.

Moths love grease spots too. That's why articles ready for storing should be dry-cleaned or laundered first.

Moth balls on a hanger. Drill two or three small holes near top of wooden-hanger beam. Press moth balls into holes and fix in place with strips of tape, so they won't fall out as they grow smaller. Pierce the tape with pinholes.

BEST SHOE FORWARD

Shoe-buying tip. One shoe salesman points out that it's best to shop for new shoes late in the afternoon, not in the morning. Reason: your feet spread as the days wears on, especially in hot weather, and if you do a lot of standing or walking.

Another tip. Since one foot is often a trifle larger than the other, buy the size that fits the larger foot. If necessary put an inner sole or a pad in the shoe of the smaller foot.

Double the life of your shoes by changing them daily. It's the airing between wearings that prevents perspiration from rotting the leather.

A shine in time preserves shoe leather and extends wear. Shine shoes before you wear them, and shine regularly thereafter.

Slippery shoe soles. You won't risk sliding around on those new shoes if you sandpaper the soles. Especially worth doing with a baby's new shoes. Or try this: rub a little linseed oil on the sole.

Silence squeaky shoes by piercing several small holes through the sole just in back of the ball of the foot.

Watch out for "builder-uppers." The shoe-repair man who fixes extra-worn sections of shoe sole by building it up beyond original thickness is the wrong man for your family's shoes. Such work is no money-saver. It just throws the shoe, and the wearer's posture, out of line, and can lead to serious problems.

Powder puffs make wonderful shoe-polish applicators. Keep one inside the can of wax shoe polish, where it won't dry out.

Lemon juice as a shoeshine works wonders. Spread a few drops on black or smooth, tan-leather shoes, then rub briskly with soft cloth. Gives elegant sheen.

Don't discard hardened shoe polish. Renew its usefulness by softening it with a little turpentine.

Substitute shoe polish. Use a little paste floor wax when you run out of shoe polish. Can be used on light or dark shoes because the wax color is neutral.

To clean shoebrushes, soak them in warm sudsy water to which a few drops of turpentine have been added.

Leather beautifier. Luggage, belts, chairs, and plain kid-leather shoes can be kept new-looking and clean by rubbing them with egg whites beaten to stiffness.

Simple leather-goods dye. To darken light tan-leather articles, such as belts, shoes, etc., rub with cloth dipped in ammonia. Gives a deep brown finish. Apply uniformly, so finish won't be spotty.

How to waterproof shoes. Apply hot ski wax to the leather, then rub in briskly with a stiff brush. After the wax is set, rub with a cloth. Keeps leather rainproof and springy.

Keep suede shoes new by rubbing them with a piece of stale rye bread or a rubber sponge after each wearing.

Stained suede shoes are easy to clean. First brush them to remove all dust particles, then hold the shoe over a steam-kettle spout long enough to raise the nap but not long enough to get the shoes wet. (A steam iron is wonderful for this too.) Brush the nap with a soft brush and let the shoes dry before wearing them again.

Rain spots on suede. Rain spots will disappear quickly from suede shoes, bags, or hats if rubbed gently with an emery board such as is used in manicuring.

Stained kid shoes. Ordinary cuticle remover will usually do away with spots on kid shoes when regular cleaning fluid isn't handy. Moisten a cloth with it and rub over the spots, which disappear quickly.

Patent-leather shoes won't crack in cold weather, and they'll look lots better, if you rub a little petroleum jelly (Vaseline) over the surface, then polish with a dry cloth.

Clean fabric shoes, such as those made of satin, linen, etc., by rubbing them with a cloth dipped in a cleaning fluid.

Keep white oxfords white by preventing the metal eyelets on the laces from discoloring the leather. Do this by coating the eyelets with a dab of colorless shellac.

If your white shoes have dark heels, apply coat of colorless nail polish to the heels. Allow to dry thoroughly. This prevents white cleaner from rubbing off on the dark surface, and a damp cloth is all you need to remove any that spills over onto heels.

Clean white shoes neatly. Make mask out of cardboard cut in shape of shoe sole. Keeps soles free from cleaning material.

Gold, silver, and kid slippers tend to tarnish with exposure to air when not worn. To keep them glamorous and untarnished, wrap them after each wearing in black tissue paper or discarded black socks.

Mildew on leather shoes can be removed. Mildew, which might form if shoes haven't been worn for some time and the storing area is not dry, should be rubbed with petroleum ointment. The marks will disappear quickly.

Shoestring tip. When the metal tips come off the laces, dip the ends into hot paraffin and twist them, or harden tip ends with a little nail polish.

READY FOR A RAINY DAY

Raincoats: waterproof vs. water-repellent. Waterproof garments (plastic, rubber, oilskin) give greater protection but are likely to be uncomfortable in warm weather, since they're airtight. Underarm ventilation may help. Water-repellent coats have the advantage of doubling as topcoats in fair weather. And many of them, especially women's coats, are very stylish.

Dry waterproof coat at room temperature. Sunlight or direct heat tends to crack some raincoat materials. Hang coat from collar strap rather than on hanger, to avoid stretching out of shape or deterioration at points of contact. This is especially necessary for rubberized types.

Rubber footwear will last longer without cracking if, when not in use, it's kept standing erect by inserting rolls of cardboard. Laundry-shirt cardboards are excellent for the purpose.

21

Laundering, Cleaning, Ironing

LABORATORY-TESTED DIRECTIONS FOR TAKING BETTER CARE OF FABRICS

Fabric, like human skin, deteriorates with dirt. Just as dirt-clogged pores cause skin blemishes, so dirt or perspiration lodged in fabric fiber weakens the threads and damages the texture. You keep fabrics healthy simply by keeping them clean. Let fabrics "breathe." Periodic airings help preserve most materials. Cottons can take the sun in varying degrees. White is always safer in the sun than colored materials of any kind. Silks, rayons, fiber blends are better off in the shade and should not be left outdoors too long.

Follow washing directions. Manufacturers are now required to print washing directions on labels permanently affixed to garments. Follow these directions carefully. Manufacturers spend a fortune in laboratory tests and research to give you the most accurate directions for cleaning your wearables and household fabrics. Lengthen fabric life, save money, avoid disappointment by using this valuable information.

Laundry reminder. Most clothes hampers are too

small for large articles of family wash. Fasten memo inside the hamper cover to remind you of bedspreads, curtains, etc. Scotch tape will hold note in place and is easily removed.

If you have a laundry basket, line it with oilcloth or plastic sheeting to protect your wash from soiling or discoloration. Cut one piece to fit the bottom, another to line the sides. Make the side lining wide enough to allow about 2 inches to fold over the edge of the basket.

New things for old. Even the best of fabrics eventually wears out, so make a discard pile when sorting your wash. If that sheet or shirt seems ready for retirement, save the "fare" another trip to the laundry would cost. Salvage the fabric by making it into handkerchiefs, underwear, sun suits, house cloths, and other usefuls.

For best laundering results, sort clothes by grouping thus:

1. White cottons and linens with fast-color pastel cottons.

2. Dark, fast-color cottons and linens.

3. Fabrics requiring special care (wools, silks, rayons, nylons, etc.)

Do the less-soiled articles first, follow with the more heavily soiled pieces.

When sorting clothes before they go into washer, empty the pockets, examine for spots, stains, torn areas. Rips should be mended before washing, to prevent more tearing. Take off all removable trims and shoulder pads.

Cut laundering time. Brush off all loose dirt from surfaces inside pockets and trouser cuffs. Pretreat heavily soiled areas by use of brush dipped in soap or special detergent suds. Avoid overloading washing machine.

A few minutes can prevent many laundry accidents.

Take time to close zippers so they won't catch on other articles and rip them. Mend rips, secure loose buttons, replace missing snaps, buttons, and other fastenings beforehand.

Protect the snaps. Have mercy on snap bindings. Fasten them together before putting through the wringer and they'll come out the way they went in.

HANDLE WITH CARE

Most woolens and silks may be laundered successfully if not exposed to excessive heat or strong detergents. If still soiled after brief washing, it is best to wash again, for a short period, in fresh suds. Rinse twice in water of same temperature as wash water. Press out moisture by gently squeezing. Do not wring. Roll in bath towel. (Check fabric at time of purchase. Don't try to wash it unless label recommends it.)

When washing sweaters, sew buttonholes together first, so they won't stretch during laundering.

Your hand-knit garments will stay in shape with home care. Wash in mild suds, then pat into proper size and shape. Dry thoroughly. When dry, hold steam iron an inch above garment, then move slowly back and forth over entire surface until steam penetrates it thoroughly, never actually touching the garment with the iron.

To wash corduroy, use lukewarm water and mild suds. Lift up and down in the water. Rub badly soiled parts with a very soft brush or with the palm. Rinse in clear water, then hang up wet without squeezing or wringing out the water. While drying, shake occasionally. When thoroughly dry, raise the nap by stroking with a soft brush in the same direction as the ribs run. An automatic dryer is ideal for drying corduroy, fluffs up the nap as it dries.

Handkerchiefs come out whiter and stay fresh longer if you place a little borax in the laundry water. Borax gives fabric just enough extra body to withstand soiling too quickly.

Whiten discolored handkerchiefs by immersing them in cold water to which you've added a pinch of cream of tartar.

Dainty lingerie and blouses should be hand-washed without soaking. If shoulder straps, band, hems, etc., are more soiled than rest of garment, pretreat with soft hand brush and mild suds.

Laundering of small lace things. To keep from tearing the dainty threads, put collars, cuffs, and other small pieces of fine lace in jar containing lukewarm suds. Shake the lace around in the jar, then empty it and refill with clear water. Return the lace and rinse by shaking the jar again. Rinse several times, until water is clear. Remove and roll the lace in a bath towel until almost dry. Then press gently with a warm (not hot) iron.

Best cleansing agents for fine fabrics and hosiery. Mild soap (in soft or softened water) or mild synthetic detergent (in hard or soft water).

Anti-snag suggestions. When washing stockings, remove all your rings other than a plain band. If your fingernails are razor-sharp, better use thin rubber gloves.

White nylon won't yellow from washing to washing if you use bluing when laundering nylon shirts, blouses, underthings, and the like.

To wash leather gloves (when washable) use lukewarm water and mild soap, leaving some soap in the glove to keep the leather soft. Don't rinse too much.

When washing doeskin or chamois gloves, add a few drops of olive oil to the water. Keeps gloves soft and pliant.

Roll gloves off your hands after washing, don't pull them off. Pulling stretches the glove fingers.

To wash feather pillows. Swish them around in the washtub or bathtub in lukewarm water and mild suds. Neither soak nor scrub the pillows. Rinse gently in clear lukewarm water by swishing them around again. Hang outdoors to dry in a spot that is shady and breezy, or dry them in your automatic dryer. Caution: don't overdry.

10 TRICKS IN WASHING BLANKETS

Your blankets will be soft, fluffy, and really clean if simple laundering rules are observed:

1. Select a wash day, if you haven't an automatic dryer, when the sun isn't too hot and the outdoor temperature is above freezing.

2. Measure the blanket.

3. Go over soiled binding areas with soft brush dipped in warm mild suds and water.

4. Dissolve soap or detergent in warm washing water before putting in blanket, if this is possible with your washer. If not, and washer has a soap dispenser at the top, don't add soap or detergent until blanket is wet through.

5. Wash only 1½ minutes, let rinse, and spin-dry 3 minutes.

6. Measure blanket again after washing and brush to its original size.

7. Two parallel, taut lines are better than one for blanket drying. Don't fold blanket or use clothespins. For dryer drying, add several dry bath towels with the blanket. They act as buffers and speed drying. Don't let blanket become completely dry, regardless of drying method, line or machine.

8. When blanket is almost dry, stretch again and brush the nap all over, on both sides of the blanket, with a stiff brush.

9. *Final step.* Press the binding with warm iron and pressing cloth.

10. *Blanket trick.* The next time you wash your wool blanket try: to the final rinse water add 1 tablespoon of household ammonia. This makes the blanket really fluffy and raises its nap so that it looks and feels like new.

COLOR CARE

Even color-fast fabrics need care in handling. The enemies of color-fastness are: excessively hot water, extended exposure to the rays of the sun, and soaking.

Color-fast articles may lose a little dye in the first laundering. Wash each piece separately the first time, so you won't chance dye transfer to other launderables.

Art of laundering colored garments: Never soak them; the colors may bleed or run. The danger is the same if you leave them lying wet. Don't dry colored fabrics in the sun, as they made fade. Prints or colors should not be ironed in double thicknesses. To avoid streaks and wanderlust colors, don't hang colored garments or iron them while too damp.

Set with salt. Common table salt is good for setting most colors, but Epsom salts are better for washing and rinsing delicately colored materials. Dissolve 1 teaspoonful of the salts to each gallon of water. The most delicate shades will not run or fade.

To make bright colors stay bright. When laundering colored garments, prevent them from graying by adding a tablespoon of vinegar to the next-to-the-last rinse.

Black and blue. When washing black or navy-blue lingerie, add a teaspoon of bluing to the water. This preserves the dye far longer than laundering in plain water.

Don't weep over faded curtains. Renew them by putting a tint dye in the washing machine with the soap or detergent. They also dye more evenly than when dipped.

HANGING HINTS

Hang 'em right. They'll wear longer, iron easier. Hang clothing on line at the strongest part: men's shirts, women's dresses, by the hems; shorts by waistband; men's cotton knit shirts by shoulders; socks and stockings by toes. Avoid hanging any articles by their corners.

For pillowcases, towels, etc., turn about 6 inches over the line and pin. Hang sheets over line with hems together, after shaking them out straight. (To help smooth out sheets, run your fingers down selvage edge while folding.)

Their place in the sun. White clothes dry well in sunshine. Colored clothes are less likely to fade if hung in the shade.

Slow clothes drying preserves color in garments much better than quick-drying methods.

Prevent colored clothes from fading by hanging them wrong side out after laundering.

Sheets won't wrinkle when drying if you hang them on the line dripping wet. The weight of the water pulls them down and practically does the ironing and straightening for you.

Remember to dry all curtains in the shade. Direct sunlight will weaken most curtain fabrics.

Woolens will hate you if you dry them in cold temperature. To keep them soft and pliant, let them dry in a warm atmosphere.

Hang slacks or trousers by the cuffs when they are drying. Weight of the wet garment will take out most of the wrinkles and reduce ironing time.

Two life savers for blankets. Never hang out to dry when the winds are strong. Never hang out in real cold weather.

Blankets won't shrink if, after washing, you dry them on curtain stretchers.

Stockings won't get tangled on an outside clothesline on a windy day if you drop one or two marbles in each stocking before hanging out to dry. The marbles will provide enough weight to stop the wind from tangling the hose but not enough to pull the stockings out of shape.

Avoid humid-weather mildew. Don't leave any dampened articles out longer than 24 hours in damp weather. If you don't plan to iron right away, allow articles to dry completely; sprinkle when ready. Or keep them in your home freezer or refrigerator, after sprinkling, wrapped in plastic sheeting or enclosed in a zippered plastic laundry bag.

New wooden clothespins have longer life if you pour boiling water over them and let them stand until the water is cold. Toughens them and prevents splitting.

Clothesline antifreeze. Does your laundry freeze to the line in winter? Prevent this by dipping a cloth in strong salt-water solution and wiping the line with it. A little salt in the last rinse water will also help.

Rustproof the clothesline. If yours is a wire clothesline your worst enemy is rust. Disarm the enemy with a nice coat of white varnish at least once a year, preferably in the spring. If the line has already started to rust, sandpaper the rust spots, then use two coats of varnish.

You won't have to keep bending over or move back and forth when hanging up your wash if you'll keep clothespins in a large towel pinned at its ends or in an inexpensive clothespin bag hung over the line. Another trick is to wear an apron with deep pockets and fill them with clothespins before you begin to hang out your wash.

Your hands won't get chilled and stay that way while

hanging out clothes in cold weather if you keep a hot-water bottle among the clothes in the basket.

Save your energy when hanging out clothes. Be sure clotheslines are strung at proper height for you. Place clothesbasket on stool or rack.

MORE ABOUT RIGHT DRYING

Unroll garments immediately after towel drying. Leaving them rolled up for any length of time may cause rot, mildew, and other damage.

Streaks will be avoided and moisture will evaporate evenly if you'll dry silk stockings on damp towels.

Washable knit woolens will keep their shape if dried by blocking back to shape on special stretchers. Never put them in automatic dryer.

Knitted garments should never be hung over a line or fastened with clothespins. Let them dry flat and they'll keep their shape.

If you're in a hurry to use the sweater you washed, place it in a bath towel and press out excess moisture with a rolling pin.

To make sure knitted mittens and sweaters go back to their original size after laundering, outline them with chalk on a galvanized window screen before laundering. Then stretch back to indicated size, when washed, by pinning down with small nails.

A washed sweater will not stretch if you rinse it in a colander and squeeze out the excess water very gently.

If you haven't a form on which to stretch washed gloves, use an old curling iron. It will do the job of stretching the fingers before they are thoroughly dry.

Or insert ordinary clothespins in the fingers of laundered gloves. This will prevent fingers from shrinking. This is especially true if they have been washed in the usual manner with soap and water.

A trick in washing delicate lace that insures the best

result is to wrap it around an empty milk bottle. Fasten the ends and dip the bottle up and down in soapy water. Then rinse by dipping in clear water.

No stretcher for lace curtains? You'll do all right if you'll put them back on the rods while the curtains are wet, then slip a second rod through the lower hems to weight them down.

To make a drying rack for small articles, sew spring paper clips to tape on an ordinary clothes hanger.

If you use the neighborhood laundromat, take a plastic pillowcase to tote home your damp clothes. They'll stay nicely damp until you get ready to iron them.

TIPS FOR IRONING

When ironing fine fabrics, don't use too hot an iron. Hurts the fabric, sometimes badly.

Tablecloth tips. To give a smart professional look to your tablecloths, remember to press the center crease only. All other folds are best made by hand, since ironed creases don't lie flat on the table.

So the fabrics won't split, occasionally change the creases from halves to thirds when ironing tablecloths and other large, flat pieces.

To keep linens neat, insert a piece of cardboard, the size of the folded article, between the folds of each piece. Then, when you remove one article, the others are not wrinkled or disturbed.

To iron embroidery properly, turn it face down on a Turkish towel, then press on the wrong side. Brings out the depth, instead of flattening it. Use the same method for braided trimming.

Steam iron keeps accessories and high-fashion garments looking lovely longer. Velvet, velveteen, corduroy, and suede, all high in the fashion picture, are pile fabrics. Dresses, coats, hats, bags, and even shoes of these materials will keep their attractive finish longer with steam treatment. Hold steam iron just above fabric and allow steam to penetrate and raise the nap.

Distilled water is best for steam irons. If you run out of it and have the kind of refrigerator that requires defrosting, collect the defrosting water in a bowl or pan to use in your steam iron.

Steam bath keeps velvet new-looking. Steaming velvet is the easiest way to remove wrinkles and to lift crushed parts. Place the velvet garment on a hanger in a steamy bathroom for an hour, then let it dry. Be sure it hangs free, perhaps from a shower bar, so that nothing touches it until the velvet is entirely dry. Small garments or velvet pieces may be steamed over the spout of a teakettle.

No shine wanted, thank you. When pressing woolen materials with a damp cloth, don't iron until the fabric is completely dry, for this causes shine. Press quickly, then allow the steam to rise. This brings up the nap marvelously.

Collar shiny? Sponge it first with vinegar, then press on the wrong side. No more shine.

Your dark cottons won't pick up lint from ironing board if you use this trick. Before starting to iron, go over the cover with a damp cloth or sponge, a wide piece of cellophane tape, or some adhesive tape wound around your hand, sticky side out.

When ironing double thicknesses, such as collars, cuffs, pockets, hems, iron first on the wrong side, then on the right side.

To prevent wrinkling clothes while ironing, do the small parts first, in this order: trimmings, collar, sleeves, back bodice, front bodice. Skirt part of dress should be the last.

Bias-cut skirts, dresses, will never develop wavy hemline if properly ironed with the weave of the cloth.

In pressing a pleated skirt, keep the pleats flat by

using a loop of string attached to a weight object. Press up to the string and then remove it before finishing.

Pin before you pleat. To iron pleated skirts, first press hem on wrong side, then on right. Place on ironing board and pin pleats, at intervals of 3 or 4 inches, to the board pad. Be sure not to catch the fabric where pins will show. Iron from the top to the bottom of the skirt. Remove the pins as you go; do not iron over them.

Another neat trick for pressing pleated skirts: place a sheet of sandpaper, rough side up, on the ironing board, to hold pleats in position. When pleats are formed, remove the paper, to avoid making impressions in the cloth.

To avoid ridges when pressing heavy seams, slip strips of paper under the loose ends before spreading a damp cloth over the area.

Scorches not always a tragedy. If you've scorched an article lightly, lay a piece of wet cloth over the scorched spot and iron over it several times. Scorch often disappears, or almost does.

Man's white shirt, when scorched, should be sponged with a cloth dipped in peroxide, then ironed again, over the blemished area, with a clean dry cloth over it.

Scorch on cottons may be removed by wetting the spot with water, then covering it with a thick paste made of starch and water. Let it remain on until dry, then use a clean cloth and peroxide to sponge it off. Press the article again and hang it in the sun for several hours.

Scorched linens. If linen scorches during ironing, cut an onion in half and rub the flat side over the mark, Then soak the linen in cold water for several hours.

Scorched woolens. To remove the blemish, wet the spot and then rub dry cornstarch over it. Brush off the cornstarch when article is dry.

TIPS THAT LIGHTEN LABOR

You needn't get tired ironing. Sit down on the job. If you buy a new ironing board, get an adjustable one and regulate it to the height of your chair. If you use a stand-up board, sit on a stool that is high enough to bring you up to height of board. Be sure the chair or stool has a proper back rest to avoid fatigue. Save steps, too, by placing a board near the table for flat-work and by having a small clothesrack handy for skirts, blouses, etc.

You'll be even less tired if you use an ironer, which speeds up the work. You need only a little practice before you'll be as adept at running an ironer as you are at using your other household appliances.

Save money you'd spend for tailor's services with new "steam and dry" type of iron. You'll recover the purchase price many times over. Steam section will do wonders for woolens. Simple button switch to "dry" provides the best method for ironing linens, heavy cottons, silk, and rayon.

Don't take chances with frayed ends of extension cords. Wrap several rubber bands over the frayed ends, to avoid a short circuit when ironing, or possible further damage.

Prevent breaks in the insulation of an iron cord at the bends where it hangs over the ironing board, or at the wall outlet, by wrapping with cellulose tape at these points.

No crossed wires. Fasten a large blanket pin to the side of the ironing board, put the iron cord through the pin, and it will slip freely back and forth as you iron, without tangling or getting in your way.

Look at cord-minders too. These clamp on your ironing board, hold the cord a couple of feet above the board, out of the way when you iron.

If your iron sticks during pressing, add a small lump of butter or lard to the starch and the iron will move smoothly.

Remove starch that has collected on your iron. Rub the hot iron over a piece of brown paper on which you've sprinkled salt.

The ironer shoe may occasionally have a little starch stuck to it. You can remove it with a mild abrasive or fine steel wool, but treat it gently.

Keep pressing cloths in a cloth pocket tacked to the ironing board so you won't have to chase around looking for the cloths.

Suspend a whiskbroom underneath your ironing board so that it will always be handy when you have to press garments that have not been brushed.

Sponge rubber is kind to your feet. When special jobs make it necessary to stand while ironing, stand on sponge-rubber mat. You won't get nearly as tired as usual.

If long pieces fall on the floor, try a card table underneath the ironing board and the problem is solved.

You can make a good sleeve board by rolling up several large magazines, tying at the center and ends, then padding with an old Turkish towel and slipping into a cover made of muslin.

Ironing-board holder can be improvised with a towel bar to keep the board standing upright when stored in a closet. Attach bar to wall at a height that will allow the board to be slipped under it easily. Stores board in minimum space.

Make rack for freshly ironed clothes. Twist a wire hanger into a square shape, so that hook part can be secured over the top of a door or a high shelf. You'll have a hanger rod several inches long.

Your ironer roller needs to have its cover laundered occasionally, the padding removed to give it a chance to breathe a little before you reassemble roller covering.

Allow your hand iron to cool before putting it away. Then wind the cord around it neatly, in order to get longest life from the cord.

22

Luggage

EXPERIENCE-TESTED TIPS ON HOW TO PACK PROPERLY AND HOW TO CARE FOR YOUR LUGGAGE

Smooth sailing with smooth-packed clothes. Whether you sail, fly, board the train, hop a bus, or take the wheel of your car, you travel for a purpose and must look your neatest to further that purpose. Here's the pick of the pack of packing tips.

From the bottom up, pack your suitcase with heavy items on the bottom, getting lighter as you near the top. If you haven't a separate hat and shoe case, pack your shoes first, starting with one corner. Stuff shoes with cosmetic jars, folded gloves, socks, stockings, etc. Saves space, keeps shoes shapely.

Fill out the corners and uneven spaces in your suitcases. This not only utilizes space to the fullest, but prevents your carefully packed clothes from sliding around and becoming wrinkled when carried.

Wardrobe case. Place dresses and suit coats on hangers; either cross sleeves over front or let hang down alongside seams of garment. Pin skirts to hangers and fold side panels toward center. Snap holder bar into position. Tuck hankies, gloves, hose, into corners of bottom section. Fit shoes into bottom of case near hinged side.

Is your beauty in the bag? Careless packing of toiletries and cosmetics can spoil your clothing and luggage. Safeguard the good looks of your clothing against your beauty aids. Suggestions:

Transfer the contents of breakable bottles and jars to plastic containers, or use the original containers with one of the following methods to prevent leaks: Paint a coat of colorless nail polish around the edge of the cap, or seal with wax from a candle. Even faster is the use of aluminum foil, which should be torn from the roll in sheets to fit each bottle or jar. Wrap the foil completely around the article, pressing to the contours of the container. Save the sheets for your return trip. When placing cosmetics in your luggage, try not to have any two pieces of glass touching. Tuck hairbrush, tissues, toothpaste tubes in empty spaces and be certain that nothing moves or shifts about when the luggage is carried.

For perfumes, there are handbag-size containers more practical for traveling, or stick to colognes and sachets, which are good travelers. Refillable purse vials give you an ample supply of your favorite scent and will match your billfold and key case.

If the small soap bars provided by hotels aren't to your taste, don't hesitate to carry your own, plus washcloth, with aluminum foil or a plastic bag to "fence in" the dampness on return.

Last-minute packing, first-minute unpacking. See that your clothes spend as little time in the suitcase as possible. While you may pack shoes, toilet articles, lingerie, and sweaters as much ahead as seems convenient, leave clothes to the last. Even if you start from the house very early in the morning and must pack the night before, at least don't close your suitcase until a few minutes before you begin your journey.

Unpacking. Do this with care, as soon as possible

after reaching your destination. It's easy to get wrinkles out of woolen garments. Just put the suit or dress on a hanger, give it a damp brushing, or hang it over a tub of steaming water. Your clothing will be fresh and ready to wear in a matter of minutes.

Bring along a travel iron if you want to press something to wear at once, immediately after unpacking. Steam travel irons are particularly useful, take up very little packing space.

Use hotel beds as ironing boards for travel pressing. Simply put several thicknesses of smooth hand towels on top of the bedspread and you have an excellent surface for quick pressing as well as a convenient appliance outlet behind the bed for plugging in the iron, where bedside lighting in hotel rooms is usually found.

In this era of air travel, the weight of your luggage is more than a matter of saving your strength: it can become quite costly if you have to pay for baggage over the allowed limits. At present, on most domestic flights the limit (except for hand-held items) is two standard-sized pieces; on international flights, that limit is *44* pounds.

WOMEN—PUT IN THE NEATNESS WHEN YOU PACK YOUR BAG

Best way to pack skirts. For that important, impeccable look, start with skirt hem at one end of your suitcase, making sure that the bottom side of the skirt lies completely smoothed out. If it isn't a straight skirt, smooth out the overhang on both sides and fold back neatly over strips of tissue paper. Another strip of tissue goes under the fold-back you make with the waist extending over the other end of the suitcase. For the next skirt, start procedure from the opposite end of the suitcase, so that the thickness evens out.

Blouses show no folds if folded right—that is, at shoulders, with sleeves under the back, much as new shirts are folded. Again, as with skirts, alternate their position for level packing.

Suit jackets are stuffed shirts, really. They may be packed like shirt blouses, possibly with sleeves folded toward their front, or topside from where you stand. Stuff front with tissue paper. Or turn suit jacket inside out except for the sleeves. Fold jacket in half, tucking one shoulder inside the other. Smooth out folds at collar and lapel.

Dresses are really skirts with blouses, so start as with skirt, the hem of your dress at one end of suitcase. Place strip of tissue paper at other end and fold back the rest of the dress over it. Stuff bodice with tissue paper, fold sleeves over or under, whichever seems to leave dress in a more normal fold. Tuck some tissue under sleeve fold too.

Lingerie. Place each item on several full-length sheets of tissue paper. Roll with tissue on outside. Place lingerie so that it will be at the top of the bag.

MEN—LEAVE OUT THE WRINKLES WHEN YOU PACK YOUR BAG

Unfold shirts to full length and refold with shirttails up over front and tucked under back of collar, and you'll keep collars from crushing when packed.

Pack shirts, shoes, belts, socks, slippers snugly but not crowded.

Travel-wise ties should be folded in half crosswise, of course, then rolled from fold. Stop rolling a few inches from the tip ends. Roll tie over accordion-pleated tissue for wrinkle-proof packing.

Pack your clothes; leave out the wrinkles. For a man's suit, the best home-away-from-home is a "two-suiter," which makes packing a joy. Follow manufacturers' directions.

You're not in it when you pack your jacket. So don't button it, just overlap it as far as the cut easily allows front to lie flat. Stuff shoulders with tissue paper. Curve sleeves over side seams at armholes.

HOW TO CARE FOR LUGGAGE

For luggage care, it is most important to be absolutely certain of exactly what material covers the article; for instance, a plastic may look like leather or fabric. No one type of cleaning is best for every kind of material. Most luggage and leather-goods retailers will be happy to identify the material of an article if it is brought to a local store.

Rawhide leather (translucent, mostly white or eggshell in color, brushlike marks in irregular pattern) can be cleaned easily with scouring powder, using steel wool only for stubborn spots. Reseal pores of the leather with several coats of clear shellac or spar varnish, allowing each coat to dry before applying another. Unprotected rawhide is candy to rodents, will encourage mold or mildew.

To clean smooth leather, pigskin (in the brown or tan family, generally), and replenish oils at the same time, use saddle soap according to container directions. Lighten the color of travel-weary leathers in this class with the juice of half a lemon in a glass of water. For larger stains, such as might be caused by water, darken the entire article with thick coats of lemon oil applied for 2 or 3 days until the leather is all of the same color. To finish and protect after cleaning, use paste wax or neutral shoe polish. Preservatives sold in luggage stores are excellent. Bad scratches should be cared for by a professional repairman.

Alligator usually wipes clean with saddle soap. Paste wax or Simonize will restore the sheen.

Colored leathers, grained or smooth, may fade as do fabrics. Use only mild soapsuds and a nearly dry sponge or soft-nap cloth. Rub very gently. Neutral shoe cream is the best polish.

Coated fabric usually looks like cotton, linen, or similar fabric that has been shellacked or varnished; some all-plastic material resembles coated fabric, so be certain before you begin cleaning. Clean with a fairly strong soap or powder. Two tablespoons of household ammonia in a pint of soapy water will help lift heavy soilage. Bleach with the juice of a lemon in a quart of water. Mildew may be removed with a solution such as toluene, a solvent available in small quantities from most hardware stores. Protect against further soiling by applying several coats of self-polishing floor wax.

Fabric. Work "dry" suds into fabric carefully. Rubberized or water-proofed linings may be sponged, dried with soft cloth. Don't use cleaning fluids when fabric is bonded to a lining or backing material.

Plastic. Most plastics wipe clean with a damp cloth. Use soap for stubborn spots. Should require no waxing. Save manufacturers' directions for cleaning when purchasing new items, since new types of plastics often require different methods.

Straw or wicker hamper-type luggage (picnic kits, etc.) may be shellacked to prevent mildew. Remove fittings first.

All-fiberglass luggage of the type that has no additional covering may be wiped with a damp cloth; scratches are smoothed out with fine steel wool.

All-aluminum luggage of the type that has no additional covering is treated as plastic. Hardware stores have preparations that remove stains from aluminum, and these, rather than home experimenting, are recommended.

Combination covering. When an article is composed of more than one type of covering, treat each material separately, as outlined, being certain of positive identification before beginning.

Hardware and locks on luggage. Never oil metal parts. Seepage almost always results, staining lining with spots that can rarely be removed. If coating on metal has become scratched, or rust begins, clean carefully with fine-grade steel wool and recoat entire section of metal with colorless nail polish or clear lacquer. Do not experiment with balky or broken locks; see a repairman before your next trip.

Linings. Avoid use of water or chemicals. More often than not, linings are glued to the body of the article. Moisture and solvents will frequently cause linings to come loose. French powder cleaners will somewhat lessen oil stains. To combat occasional odors that may come from infrequent use, try keeping chlorophyll tablets in the suitcase, or sachets, or wrapped cakes of soap such as are provided by hotels.

GO FURTHER WITH WELL-STORED LUGGAGE

Never store dirty, stained, or soiled suitcase, leather goods, or brief case. Moths, vermin, mice will feast on it and the damage may be beyond repair.

If you nest cases inside one another, make sure the inner pieces are carefully wrapped in paper or luggage covers. Hardware can snag linings, and excessive humidity will promote rust, which causes permanent stains.

Store accessories in normal humidity and temperature. Too much moisture in the air can cause mildew, mold, rust. Too little moisture promotes brittleness and cracking. Use bags of dehumidifying powder in or near articles to combat excessive humidity, particularly if you live near water or in the South. A large open pan of water, replenished from time to time, will help humidify a dry atmosphere, especially if storage space must be near a furnace, radiators, or in an uninsulated attic.

Allow air to circulate. Stand luggage upright on hinged ends with a space between each case. Avoid storing cases on the floor, especially in the cellar. Instead place the cases on a plank raised a few inches on two blocks of wood or bricks. This helps prevent rust, mildew, and mold.

Protect suitcases with luggage cover or heavy paper wraps if you don't anticipate using them for a long period. Wrap small items in tissue.

Folding (traveling) garment bags provide storage for out-of-season garments. Hang them in closet or attic as regular storage bags. Protect tops against dust by making shoulder covers of paper or old plastic tablecloths, etc.

23

Spots and Stains

HOW TO REMOVE THE MOST COMMON ONES AND SAVE MANY DOLLARS IN CLEANING BILLS

With proper attention to the storage of some of the materials, and respect for them while applying them, removing spots and stains at home can be a safe procedure. But safety must be stressed. Some of the substances are flammable and/or poisonous, and others are at least harmful to the skin. You cannot afford to take the slightest chance, especially if there are children around the home.

For about the cost of dry-cleaning a single garment, you can own a handy kit containing these most often needed:

1. *White vinegar,* for dissolving acid stains.

2. *Ammonia,* for "spotting" that requires an alkali.

3. *Neutral detergent;* there are numerous good ones at your grocery store.

4. *Glycerine,* a wet-cleaning lubricant.

5. *Petroleum jelly or white mineral oil,* for use as a dry-cleaning lubricant.

6. *Hydrogen peroxide,* for stains that require a mild bleach.

7. *Amyl acetate* (banana oil), available at your drugstore.

8. *Mild castile soap,* available at your drugstore.

9. *Grease solvent;* there are several to choose, both by chemical names or by trade names. All are poisonous and some are flammable, so follow directions carefully.

10. *Chlorine bleach,* for stains requiring a strong bleach.

11. *White blotting paper,* or paper toweling.

12. *A small, stiff-bristled brush.*

Don't try home cleaning methods on these fabrics: rayon taffeta, heavily sized nets, spun rayons that contain resin or sizing, flock-printed fabrics. In these cases your dry cleaner has better resources than you could possibly command.

Help your dry cleaner do his best. When taking a stained garment to your dry cleaner, be sure to attach a note indicating stained area and explaining type of stain if you know its origin.

DO'S AND DON'T'S THAT SAVE FABRICS, DOLLARS AND DISAPPOINTMENT

Play it safe. Work in good light. And be sure no flames are present when using flammable solvents.

Test resistance of fabric colors to the cleansing agent being used. Find inconspicuous area in seam or inner layer of double facing, etc., on which to make test. If a separate swatch of fabric happens to be available, so much the better.

Protect your hands, and do a better job when dry-cleaning your own dainties, by using a wire potato masher as a plunger to gently force liquid through the cloth. Or buy a special little cleaning machine equipped with its own no-hands plunger.

Work as quickly as possible. Repeated brief applications of cleansing materials are best. Using too strong a solution and permitting it to remain on stain for too long a time can damage the fabric.

When directions call for small amount of cleansing agent, such as ammonia, vinegar, etc., stretch stained area over a bowl or beaker containing cold water and apply with eye dropper.

Use alkalies warily. Alkalies, especially strong or caustic soaps, should never be used on animal fibers. For instance, alkalies are generally destructive to wool and silk.

Mineral acids are harmful to vegetable fibers like cotton, linen, rayon, etc. Sulfuric and hydrochloric acid are mineral. Nitric and oxalic acid will also attack cellulose fibers if dried into material.

After using any substance for stain removal, rinse it thoroughly from the article before drying or pressing.

To prevent permanent fiber damage, avoid excessive friction, especially with silk and rayon. Apply the necessary stain removers to these fabrics with a soft brush. Where some rubbing or other form of fabric friction is called for, especially on delicate fabrics, work on reverse side of material.

White kid gloves sometimes turn yellowish after several cleanings. Avoid this by adding a teaspoon of powdered borax to the cleaning fluid.

To bleach out dyes that have bled to other portions of garment (usually caused by excessive soaking or the use of too much alkali or acid): Start dye bleeding again. Use ammonia in the rinse water. If it bleeds on acid side, use some white vinegar in the water. In some cases you may be able to do the job by soaking in a solution of detergent and water. Continue until discoloring dye is cleared away. Then rinse thoroughly in cold water to loosen any remaining dye. The dye must then be set with an acid (such as vinegar), or an alkali (such as ammonia), in water. In some cases salt in the water will set the dye. The use of acid or alkali depends on what caused the dye to bleed in the first place. If it bled with an acid, set the dye with an alkali-and-water-solution, and vice versa. For example, if dye bleeding is caused by soap (an alkali), clear away the dye with an alkaline solution (such as ammonia and water), then set the fabric's original dye after rinsing with a slight acid-water solution (such a white vinegar and water).

TERMS USED IN DIRECTIONS FOR STAIN REMOVAL

Bleeding. Loss of dye. If fabric is not color-fast, the dye may be loosened from the fabric under certain conditions (as when soaked in water). The color then is said to "bleed."

Feathering out. A way of treating stains that avoids a spotting ring on fabric. Whether you wet-clean or dry-clean, the outer edge of the saturated area must be allowed to dry gradually toward the center, to eliminate the ring. Do this by wiping the outer edges vigorously with dry cloth. A hand blower or hair dryer is helpful in drying the outer edge before a ring develops.

Flushing out. Removing stain by working it free from fabric by brushing, rinsing, etc.

Sizing. A stiffening agent used in fabrics. Sometimes fabric itself is weighted with resinous or other substances. Sometimes it comes in separate stiffening fabrics, such as buckram, employed to give extra firmness to collars, facing, belts, etc.

Spotting. The actual process of removing spots and stains. Methods of "spotting" include:

Lubrication. Using cleaners with oil bases.

Solvent action. Use of so-called "wet" and "dry" solutions for dissolving stains.

Mechanical action. Scraping, rubbing, brushing, etc.

Wet-cleaning and dry-cleaning. Terms to indicate whether a specfic stain responds to treatment by so-called "wet" or "dry" cleansing agents. Wet cleansers are liquids, the most important being water. Dry ones contain no actual moisture, even when in liquid form.

SPECIFIC SPOT-REMOVAL DIRECTIONS

Acids (Wet-clean). First rinse with cold water. If any solid substance is imbedded in stain, you may have to flush it out with a fairly concentrated solution of neutral detergent. If acid is strong mineral type (such as hydrochloric or sulfuric battery acid), follow cold-water treatment with application of ammonia to completely neutralize it. Such strong acids will quickly damage cotton, rayon, etc. Wool is more resistant, but sufficient acid concentration can also damage it. Color changes caused by acid stain can usually be neutralized with household ammonia and water.

Adhesive tape (Dry-clean). Usually easy to remove with grease solvent or some amyl acetate. After treating stain, rub rather vigorously with clean cheesecloth to avoid ring.

Alcoholic beverages (Wet-clean). Rinse immediately from fabric with cold water, especially if fabric is cellulose acetate, because acetate yarns bleed profusely in alcohol and loss of color often results. Since alcohol is readily soluble in water, it will come out easily. If other food substances are present, remove with neutral detergent.

Ammonia stains (Wet-clean). Ammonia may bleed dye or cause color change. Color changes can be corrected by applying white vinegar and water to affected area.

Axle grease (Dry-clean). Unless grease spot contains dirt, a grease solvent does the trick quickly. Should stain appear to be rather heavy, lubricate first with white mineral oil, then flush from fabric with grease solvent.

Blood (Wet-clean). If fabric can withstand plain water, soak it first in a pan or bowl of cold water, or between two wet towels. Add about ½ teaspoon neutral detergent to soaking bath. When using towels, apply concentrated solution of detergent to the stain itself, this usually being enough to remove it. If stain still persists, apply small amount of household ammonia to area and rub between your fingers (unless fabric is acetate), or use back of comb to help break up stain. Flush from fabric as necessary. Hydrogen peroxide can also be effective, if fabric can stand such bleaching.

Bluing (Wet-clean). Soak stain in solution of water to which you've added ½ teaspoon of neutral detergent and about 1 ounce of household ammonia. Soak for about an hour if color of fabric permits, then launder. If any of the stain remains, next step is bleaching. For rayon, cotton, or acetate, use weak solution of chlorine bleach. For silk or wool, use hydrogen peroxide.

Butter (Dry-clean). Sponge out with grease solvent. When dry (a matter of seconds), sponge out remaining traces of stain that may be water-soluble (such as salt) with solution of water and neutral detergent.

Candle wax (Dry-clean). Scrape off surface wax with dull knife. Heat small amount of grease solvent by placing a little bottle of it in a pan of hot water. Place towel under stain, then apply the warm solvent, flushing out stain onto the towel. Use of small brush to help break up the stain will speed removal. Sometimes such stains can also be removed by placing stained fabric between two pieces of blotting paper and pressing with warm iron.

Candy (Wet-clean). Since mostly sugar, candy stains are usually easy to remove by sponging out with plain water. In more stubborn cases a neutral detergent in the water will help. (See also directions for Chocolate Stains.)

Carbon paper (Dry-clean). Sponge with grease solvent. To remove remaining traces of dyestuff, flush out with a solution of water, detergent, and small amount of ammonia.

Carrot juice (Wet-clean). In washables this stain usually comes out in laundering. If not, treat stained area with solution of water and neutral detergent.

Catsup (Wet-clean). Remove as soon as possible, because age makes this one hard to budge. First flush as much of stain as possible in fairly concentrated solution of neutral detergent and water. Lubricate remaining portions of stain with glycerine, working it in with blunt edge of knife or back of comb. Then flush again with detergent-and-water solution.

Chewing gum (Dry-clean). Remove heavy portions of gum with blunt edge of knife or similar object. Then sponge area with either grease solvent or amyl acetate. The gum will loosen itself from fabric and remainder can be rolled off with finger or blunt-edged instrument. If some stubborn residue remains, keep saturating area until gum is all dissolved and rinsed from garment. Afterward, rub area thoroughly with dry cloth and allow to dry.

Chocolate (Wet-clean). First apply grease solvent to stain to remove oils present in chocolate. When area has dried, apply solution of water and detergent. Unless fabric is taffeta or satin, flex area slightly between fingers to help break up stain, or tamp it with brush. Then launder garment or flush stained area with water and wipe with dry cloth, working to break up wet edge of stain, to prevent ring from developing. This is called "feathering out."

Cocoa (Wet-clean). Follow same directions as for

chocolate, except that cocoa stain is likely to be more deeply imbedded and require more work.

Cod-liver oil (Dry-clean). Treat without delay; this oil tends to oxidize fast. If freshly spilled, flushing out with grease solvent is likely to be enough. Otherwise lubricate stain with a little white mineral oil or Vaseline. Work into stain with back of comb or blunt edge of knife. Then flush out lubricant again with grease solvent. If any trace of stain remains, use soap and ammonia, unless color is likely to bleed.

Coffee (Wet-clean). Treat as soon as possible, because tannin compounds in coffee are impossible to remove once they've dried. If possible, soak stained area in bowl of warm water and neutral detergent solution. Watch to detect quickly if any bleeding of dye occurs. If it does, soak immediately in cold water and stop working on it. If no dye bleeds, soak in original solution, then flex between fingers (except taffeta or satin, etc.). If necessary, work some glycerine into stain and soak again. Avoid hot water and alkalies (such as soap). On white cotton, rayon, or acetate, use bleaching solution of chlorine to remove remaining traces. Then wash, if fabric is dyefast. For wool and silk, bleach with a milder agent such as hydrogen peroxide (drugstore variety).

Cooking oil (Dry-clean). Follow same directions as for linseed oil.

Crayon (Dry-clean). Sponge out stained area with grease solvent, flushing stain out onto towel placed under it. If necessary to lubricate stain, use some Vaseline or white mineral oil. Then flush area again. In washables, if traces remain, try removing with soap and ammonia, color permitting.

Cream (Wet-clean). Follow same directions as for ice cream.

Egg stains (Wet-clean). Scrape any caked-on residue from fabric with dull edge of knife. Apply cold water and neutral detergent and allow to soak in such a solution for few minutes, depending on tendency of dye to bleed. Brush, or flex between fingers to loosen particles imbedded in fabric. If necessary, lubricate area with glycerine or neutral detergent (in heavily concentrated form). Then apply soap or neutral detergent to stain, plus ammonia. Tamp with brush or flex between fingers. Then flush area, wipe it dry, or launder garment.

Fish slime (Wet-clean). This is a concentrated albumen stain and can be very difficult to remove, impossible on certain resin-treated or sized fabrics. Soak stained area immediately in pan containing solution of water with some neutral detergent and about a spoonful of salt. Soak about 10 minutes and flex slightly between fingers or tamp with brush. Rinse in plain cold water. Should stain remain, further home treatment is not advisable. Send to dry cleaner, identifying the stain.

Floor wax (for washables and non-washables). Laundering will remove most of wax stain. Remove leftover traces with grease solvent spotting treatment.

Fruit and fruit juices (Wet-clean). Brown or tan stains resulting from fruit juice are due to sugar in the fruit. Often stains don't show at once, but the stain may set as fruit sugar dries and caramelizes (turning brown), the way sugar does under high heat. Once caramelized, such stains become difficult to treat, and practically impossible on wool. Flush stain as soon as possible in a solution of water and neutral detergent. Soaking may also help. If stain remains, try few drops of white vinegar, then flush again in detergent and water. Don't use high heat on the stain, since this speeds up caramelization and only sets the stain faster.

Gelatin stains (Wet-clean). Normally laundering will remove such stains, provided water is not over 100° F.

Hot suds and rinses tend to set rather than to remove stain.

Glue or mucilage (Wet-clean). Soak out stain in hand-warm water and neutral detergent, then apply some household ammonia and tamp with brush or flex between fingers. Rinse, then wipe area with dry cloth.

Grass stains (Wet-clean). Test fabric to see if it will withstand alcohol by applying some to hidden area (such as the seam). If this is all right, use alcohol to remove green color, then lubricate area with concentrated detergent solution and flush both alcohol and detergent out of fabric with cold water. Next apply few drops of household ammonia to stain and at the same time work in more detergent solution. Flush again with cold water and launder if possible. Otherwise wipe area with dry cloth and let dry.

Gravy (For washables and non-washables). Because greases will doubtless be present in stain, remove these first by sponging area with grease solvent. Then apply some detergent solution and ammonia (or alkaline soap). Flex, or tamp with brush. Rinse in warm water.

Grease and oil (Dry-clean). Mineral oils and greases are readily soluble in dry solvent. Sponge out stained area with grease solvent, which will remove oils quite thoroughly. If water-soluble oil is also present in the stain, remove by sponging the area with solution of soap or detergent and water.

Grease spots on carpets, rugs (Dry-clean). Usually easy to remove by rubbing stained area with piece of cheesecloth slightly saturated with grease solvent. Rub over outer edges with dry cloth as spotted area dries, to prevent formation of ring. Be sure to have towel or similar absorbent material under rug and try to avoid letting solvent contact the floor, since it may affect the wood finish.

Ice cream (Wet-clean). If stained area is dry, sponge with grease solvent to remove fats. When the solvent has evaporated, apply solution of water, detergent, and few drops of ammonia directly on the stain. Work stain with back of comb or knife and flush it from fabric with cold water.

Ink: India, printer's, ball-point (Dry-clean). First put good absorbent material under stain. Then lubricate stain with Vaseline or white mineral oil. Flush lubricant and as much of stain as possible with grease solvent. Repeat until ink stops bleeding. Ball-point ink removes without much trouble. Others may take more work. Back of comb or dull knife edge helps work ink particles free and facilitates stain removal.

Iodine (Wet-clean). Quickly remove with sodium thiosulphate crystals (usually called hypo crystals), which are available at drugstores. Place some crystals in piece of cheesecloth, moisten them, and pat stained area with wet crystals. Drop of ammonia tends to speed up action, but stain usually disappears quickly anyway. Rinse with cold water and wipe with dry cloth.

Iron rust. Use either commercial rust remover (hydrofluoric acid) or get oxalic-acid crystals at drugstore. Place a few in cheesecloth, moisten, and apply to stain. After stain is removed, be sure to rinse acid completely from fabric.

Lacquer (Dry-clean). If color permits (alcohol bleeds acetate dyes), alcohol is best solvent. As lacquer softens and becomes dissolved, rinse from fabric with grease solvent. If dye bleeds with alcohol (test inconspicuous area to determine this), apply amyl acetate to stain until it tends to dissolve, then rinse with grease solvent.

Lead pencil (Wet-clean). Work glycerine or heavy detergent solution into stains with blunt-edged object. Apply few drops of ammonia and gently work into stain until it tends to dissolve, then rinse with grease stain. As stains dissolve, flush from fabric with warm water.

Leather stains (Dry-clean). Very difficult to remove. Lubricate thoroughly with white mineral oil or Vaseline, then rinse lubricated areas with grease solvent. If garment is white and washable, stains may also be treated with soap and ammonia, rubbing leather-stained areas between hands. Using chlorine bleach on the remaining traces may clear stain. Unless these methods get quick results, turn job over to dry cleaner as soon as possible.

Linseed oil (Dry-clean). Very harmful to garment, because once it has been in fabric long enough to oxidize, it's almost impossible to remove. Speed is vital. Lubricate stained area with white mineral oil or Vaseline, working into stain with blunt-edged object. Then rinse with grease solvent. Repeat if necessary. If such measures fail, give to dry cleaner.

Lipstick (Dry-clean). If stain is fresh, grease solvent treatment is often enough. Otherwise lubricate stain well with white mineral oil or Vaseline and flush with grease solvent. Try to do complete job this way. Once the lipstick dye becomes separated from the lubricant in the lipstick, its removal requires this further treatment: In a solution of water, ammonia, and detergent, soak stain for hour or two (depending on what the fabric color can stand), then work stain between fingers occasionally while soaking. Finally, rinse thoroughly in warm water.

Liquor stains: alcohol (Wet-clean). Alcohol content can be particularly damaging to acetate fabrics because it bleeds their dyes so severely. The longer stain remains, the more the damage. Sponge area immediately with solution of water and neutral detergent. If fruit juices are also present, follow procedure given for their removal after rinsing out the alcohol. It may be necessary to let your cleaner take over further spotting activity.

Machine oil This is a mineral oil, therefore soluble in grease solvent. Sponge out the stain.

Mascara (Dry-clean). Follow same directions as for lipstick stains.

Mayonnaise (Dry-clean). Follow same directions as for linseed oil.

Meat juice (Dry-clean). First sponge with grease solvent to remove grease. When dry, sponge with either a detergent and ammonia or soap and ammonia.

Mildew (Wet-clean). If garment is washable, first launder in soap-and-ammonia solution, then rinse well and dry in the sun. If color will withstand bleaching action of chlorine bleach, use that. Don't try to do job on wool or fancy fabrics. Play safe; give it to your dry cleaner.

Milk (Wet-clean). Sponge area with neutral detergent and water, then add few drops of ammonia to area and continue using detergent solution. If necessary, tamp stain with brush or work back and forth across it with blunt-edged object. For old milk stains it may be necessary to use an anzyle (such as powdered pepsin), available at drugstores. Soak in solution of water and pepsin at least 20 minutes at temperature slightly above hand-warm. After soaking, repeat above procedure. Milk stains may be impossible to remove on some resin-treated fabrics.

Mud (Wet-clean). Allow to dry. Then dry-brush as much as possible from garment. Sponge remaining mud with warm solution of water and detergent. Launder, or flush out with plain water and wipe down with dry cloth.

Mustard (Wet-clean). On washables, apply glycerine. After working it into stain, flush with detergent and water. Do not use soap. If stain remains, better let dry cleaner try. Even he, however, may not be able to eliminate yellow stain caused by a chemical in the mustard.

Nail polish (Dry-clean). Dissolves in acetone or amyl acetate. However, do not use acetone if fabric is rayon, vinyon, acetate, or nylon, since it damages them. Note: do not use nail-polish remover on above-mentioned fabrics since it, too, often contains acetone.

Oils and fats: other than cooking oils, linseed and similar oils (Dry-clean). Generally easy to dissolve in grease solvents. In severe cases lubricate stain with white mineral oil, then sponge with grease solvent.

Paraffin (for washables and non-washables). Laundering is usually sufficient. If stain persists, place towel or fold of absorbent cloth under it and sponge with grease solvent. Piece may then be rewashed as required.

Perfume (Wet-clean). Flush from fabric with solution of detergent and water as soon as possible, because alcohol in perfume will severely bleed some dyes, such as acetate. If fabric has no acetate, small amount of alcohol added to detergent solution will help. Test first for color-fastness to alcohol.

Perspiration (Wet-clean). When fresh, perspiration is acid in nature. However, bacteria act upon it quickly, turning it alkaline. For fresh stains, flush area with detergent, water, and ammonia in solution. For old stains (by now turned alkaline), use a solution of water, detergent, and vinegar. Sometimes color changes occur from either acids or alkalies. An acid or alkali will restore the color, depending on which agent originally caused the color change.

Plastic stains (Dry-clean). Follow same directions as for nail polish.

Resins (Dry-clean). Use turpentine, grease solvent, alcohol, or similar organic solvents, but be sure no flame is present anywhere near where you are working. Stain should be softened and well soaked in solvent. Work cleansing agent into stain with glass stirring rod.

If fabric has to be rubbed, use soft sponge or brush. Avoid chafing fabric (to prevent combustion).

Rouge (Dry-clean). Follow same directions as for lipstick.

Rubber stains (Dry-clean). Usually respond to treatment with grease solvent or gasoline (special cleaning type). Do not work near flame.

Salad dressing (Dry-clean). Follow same directions as for linseed oil.

Salad oil (Dry-clean). Follow same directions as for linseed oil.

Scorch (Wet-clean). If fabric is washable, launder first. Scorch itself must be removed by bleach. If fabric will withstand chlorine bleach (rayon, acetate, nylon, etc.), and if dye will also react favorably, bleach as you wash. If scorch is on wool, apply hydrogen peroxide by spray or with a cloth (in this case use rubber gloves). Then place garment so that stained area faces the sun. Watch from time to time until stain is gone. If necessary, apply more hydrogen peroxide as it dries out. If dye begins to lighten, stop procedure and rinse peroxide from fabric.

Shoe polish (Dry-clean). Liquid polish stains are usually impossible to remove, because of high tannin content. Paste-type polishes are often easily removable (especially from wool) because of lubricating agents in them. Sponge out area thoroughly with grease solvent. If necessary to lubricate stain further, use white mineral oil or Vaseline, then sponge again with grease solvent.

Soot (Wet-clean). Especially tough to remove if soot stain is wet. Soak garment or affected area in heavy solution of detergent and water to lubricate, penetrate, and flush away stain. Watch fabric colors carefully if long soaking is necessary. If severe color bleeding starts, rinse garment or spot the area with cold water. (Some salt in the water usually checks or prevents bleeding.) If bleeding takes place, don't continue; let cleaner take over. Bleaching is ineffective, because soot is primarily carbon.

Sugar syrup (Wet-clean). Follow same directions as for candy.

Tar (Dry-clean). Catch this stain as soon as possible. Remove heavy portions with blunt-edged instrument. Then sponge thoroughly with grease solvent. If natural tar lubricant has dried out, relubricate with either Vaseline or white mineral oil. Then sponge out with more grease solvent. If stain is stubborn, continue by using glycerine, soap, or a similar agent, working it into the stain. Then flush with water or launder garment. Color-fastness and washability of fabric determine which course you take.

Tea (Wet-clean). Normal washing will usually suffice, unless stain has been present a long time. If stain is stubborn, use chlorine bleach on white cotton or linen; hydrogen peroxide on silk or wool (if color will withstand the bleach).

Tin foil (for washables and non-washables). Foil from corsages can leave stains. First lubricate with white mineral oil or Vaseline, working well into stain. Then flush with grease solvent. Wipe fabric vigorously with dry cloth as solvent evaporates from it. When dry, switch to wet-cleaning by lubricating stain with glycerine or soap, then flush well with water.

Tobacco juice (Wet-clean). Lubricate with glycerine, then soak garment or stained area in solution of detergent and hand-warm water. On whites, bleaching may be necessary, chlorine bleach for cottons and synthetics, hydrogen peroxide for silk and wool. Tobacco's tannin content makes it a difficult stain to remove.

Tomato juice (Wet-clean). Follow same directions as for catsup.

Tooth paste (Wet-clean). If dry, most of it can be dry-brushed off. Otherwise, usually easy to flush off with either soap-and-water or detergent-and-water solution. Since some tooth pastes contain sodium perborate (a bleach), guard against allowing stain to damage fabric; remove quickly.

Vaseline (Dry-clean). Easy to remove with grease solvent. After sponging, wipe area dry with clean cloth.

Water spots: on taffeta (Wet-clean). If fabric shows spots, it contains considerable sizing, which creates a problem. No home method will work. Dry cleaner has certain facilities that usually solve the situation.

Wine (Wet-clean). Work on this stain as soon as possible. Apply concentrated solution of neutral detergent and some glycerine, working it into area. Allow to remain a few minutes, then sponge with clear water, about hand-warm (never hot). Flex stain between fingers while rinsing. If some color of wine remains, apply few drops of ammonia with some detergent to the stain. This may turn it from blue to pink. White vinegar will turn it back to original blue. Such a condition means that a so-called indicator dye is present and there is little you can do unless fabric can withstand bleaching.

24

Home Furnishings

HOW TO GET BETTER AND LONGER SERVICE FROM THE THINGS THAT MAKE A HOME

Some people think all knots in wood denote defects. This is not true. Knots that form an integral part of the wood are completely sound, should not be rejected. Sometimes they even make the grain pattern more attractive. However, black knots (dead-wood spots) are likely to drop out as the board weathers. Examine wood carefully.

Overheated rooms will injure your finest pieces of furniture and ruin antiques. Don't store extra table leaves in cellar or other damp areas. Avoid placing furniture against hot radiators or under open windows.

No-snag furniture. If you have any chairs that keep snagging your hosiery, sandpaper away the roughened spots, then coat with clear shellac.

Smooth-sliding drawers. To make those hard-to-budge drawers slide much more easily, put thumbtacks on the runners.

Fresh touch for dresser drawers. Empty them every so often and clean by wiping down inner surfaces with soapy cloth and rinsing with clean damp cloth. When dry, line drawers with waxed paper or plastic sheeting.

Scratchproof furniture casters. Casters will roll quietly and smoothly if rolling surfaces of the wheels are covered with adhesive tape. Ends of tape should meet but not overlap, as this would cause uneven rolling.

Casters stay put. If caster keeps slipping out, wrap a slip of adhesive tape around the stem of the caster until it fits the hole snugly. Or fill the hole with melted paraffin and then insert caster.

Piano-care hints. Extremes of temperature hurt the instrument. Keep pianos away from windows often opened in wintertime, away from radiators and steam-pipes, away from damp spots. You'll need tuning less often and the instrument will last much longer. In summertime, since the felted hammers attract moths, safe-guard them with paracrystals. Note, also, that piano keys need light to retain their sparkling whiteness, so they should not be constantly covered, and that idle pianos do not stay in good condition, so that moving parts should be exercised weekly with several hours of playing.

To clean piano keys, dip a piece of flannel in dena-tured alcohol and wipe each key carefully. Then dry at once with another piece of flannel.

Rush-bottom chairs won't develop split reeds for a long time if you apply a coat of clear shellac over the seats.

Restore loose cane seats. Cane seats loosened by too much strain quickly tighten up if you do this: Go over the seat with a rag soaked in hot water, then set the chair in the sun to dry.

Ideal care for leather furniture. When leather shows signs of soiling, wash with a thick lather of castile or saddle soap. Remove soap with damp cloth, then wipe dry. Occasionally use leather dressing to keep it pliable and prevent cracking.

To clean leather chair seats, rub each seat with half

a lemon. Polish with furniture oil, then shine up with a dry cloth.

Or shine up leather furniture by using a soft piece of cotton dipped in vinegar. First squeeze cotton almost dry, then polish.

To repair cigarette burns in upholstered furniture, select a yarn color to match material, darn hole with close stitches. Place damp cloth over spot and iron the patched area.

Beware the busy moths. Spraying is not enough precaution with over-stuffed furniture, even if you use slip covers. Remove covers once a month and check to make sure no stray moth colony has survived the spray. A few moments of effort can avoid lots of damage. Apply more mothproofing if necessary.

When pets shed. Even prize-winning dogs and cats will shed hair on the furniture. You can whisk the hairs off in record time by sliding a piece of adhesive tape very gently over the furniture surface. The hairs will stick to the tape, and your pet will be out of the "doghouse."

Even angora hairs can be removed from furniture by dabbing with a damp sponge.

FURNITURE SURFACES

Fingerprints on furniture can be removed easily with a cloth saturated in olive oil. When applying wax polish, use just as little as possible and rub until you get a surface free of film. If you do, furniture will increase in loveliness.

How to remove heat marks from table tops. Rub the unsightly white marks with a hard paraffin wax candle. Then cover with blotting paper and press with warm iron. Repeat, if necessary. Afterward, rub well with soft cloth to restore finish.

White rings vanish. Unsightly white rings on highly polished furniture (from heat, etc.) will disappear upon applying warm camphorated oil. Rub the furniture until it is dry, then polish with a clean, soft cloth.

Protect your fashionable marble-top furniture. If stains don't respond to soap and water, rub spots with a cotton pad soaked in lemon juice. Rinse surface thoroughly with clean water to prevent damage to marble. Colorless polishing wax is a good conditioner for thoroughly clean marble.

Give mahogany furniture a vinegar rinse. Restore dull or blurred finish to its original luster this way: Wring out a soft cloth in a solution of vinegar and warm water. Wipe the surface of the furniture with it and leave it on for a day or two. Then apply furniture cream or polish.

Paper stuck to table surface can damage finish unless you take this precaution: Put a few drops of oil on the paper scrap. Let it soak through for several minutes, then rub gently with a soft cloth. Paper is then easily removed without damaging wood finish.

Scratchproofer. Beautiful table tops need not be marred by scratches from the bottoms of ash trays or knickknacks if you cushion bottoms with pieces of felt cut to shape. Attach with glass cement. For very small areas use pieces of adhesive tape.

Make nicks invisible. During spring cleaning all the nicks and scratches that your furniture has accumulated during the year usually show up all at once. A furniture expert points out that you can first darken these scratches with wood stain, to get back as nearly as possible to the original color of the wood, and then apply white shellac to the scratches, one coat at a time, until they are filled.

Furniture scratches disappear. A little iodine applied to a scratch on dark furniture will nearly always erase the blemish or make it much less noticeable.

Speed up furniture polishing. Since warm polish penetrates wood pores fast, warm your bottle of polish beforehand by placing it in a pan of hot water for a little while.

Wonderful furniture polisher. An ordinary shoe buffer is a tool that's especially good for pieces with curves and molding. Soft pad gets into all uneven surfaces.

When do you wax? New pieces of furniture should be polished with wax or wax polish every two weeks. Later, once a month is enough. Wax protects surface against water or liquor marks.

Wax wise. Polish furniture or floor surface with cloth wrapped around a small sandbag. This adds weight, results in smoother work.

DRAPES, CURTAINS, AND SLIPCOVERS

Even if fabric is washable, it's best to dry-clean slip covers and draperies. Why? In washing, they may get distorted and shrink just enough not to fit well afterward. Some of the heavier fabrics and trimmings, washable-dyed though they are, may contain excess dye that will bleed.

If wash you must, make sure the material, as well as the trimmings, is indeed washable. Use only lukewarm water and only fine mild soaps. If you cleanse in a washing machine, don't let it spin too long. If a color runs while you are washing the article, rinse immediately several times in succession, until the last rinsing water is absolutely clear. Hang to dry so that deep-colored parts can't drip on lighter sections.

To press draperies. Cotton and linen may be ironed on the right side with a hot iron. Rayon should be pressed on wrong side with only a warm iron. No-iron fabrics should be rehung while still slightly damp, so they can be shaped into place by hand.

Snap those draperies. Take this cue from a young lady who sets the pinched pleats at the top of her draperies with snap fasteners. She pins in her pleats and uses a home kit for applying the snaps. Before sending her curtains to the cleaner, she can unsnap the pleats in a jiffy. When her draperies return, she resets and hangs them just as quickly.

Snap when you clean too. Fasten snaps at the bottom and part way up in an unobtrusive spot at each side of drapery panels. When cleaning, simply turn up the drapery and snaps hold the fabric off the floor when you dust it.

Put slip covers back on while still slightly damp. They'll smooth out as they dry, fit better than if you ironed them. Only the ruffles and pleats may need a bit of touching up. Even those, however, you can do after the slip cover is back on the furniture. Put a towel between the cover and furniture when you're pressing the edges of freshly laundered slip cover.

Hand laundering is the rule for sheer curtains. Easy does it. Be equally careful in hanging them to dry, in smoothing them, and finger-pressing the seams, as this will facilitate the ironing job. If it's a straight curtain, slip a rod in the hem and hang at the window to dry.

Your lovely curtains shrank in washing or cleaning? You can add length to them in several ways:

If shrinking is only hem-length, carefully rip hem, let it down, and add a false hem of material of same color and weight (even if you can't match it exactly). Or rip the heading at top, and add a false heading.

If shrinkage is more than that, add fringe the length desired (cotton fringe to cotton curtains, rayon to rayon, etc.), for a formal room. In an informal room, curtains may be lengthened by adding a band of a contrasting material at the bottom (and even at the heading if desired).

LINEN AND BEDDING

Pure linen towels are best for drying dishes. They more than make up for the small extra cost since they absorb moisture so readily and leave no lint. Watch for the seasonal "white sales" and buy them at minimum cost.

Towels should be well woven. Test this way: Hold towel up to a bright light. Light should come through in even pin points. If it's in uneven patches, the ground cloth is unevenly woven and will not wear well.

Plain white towels usually cost the least. The addition of color, embossing, or other decoration increases the price as well as laundry upkeep.

The thicker are better. Heavy bath towels are more absorbent.

Grounds for refund. Woven borders sometimes shrink more than the body of the bath towel. This cannot be determined before washing, but it does constitute a defect and should be grounds for returning the towel. Moral: save those sales slips, or buy a reputable brand.

When buying bed sheets, guard against "April fool" fabrics by testing for excess sizing. Rub a portion of the sheet between your fingers. If fine white powder comes off on your hands, look for a better quality. You'll save money in the long run because this powder (called sizing) will wash out in the first laundering.

Economy tip. Heavier muslin sheets wear much longer, tear less easily, than medium weights, cost only a trifle more.

Blue prevents yellowing. To help keep your linens from yellowing, paint the inside of your linen closet a medium shade of blue.

The thicker the blanket, the warmer. High nap is desirable, for low nap often indicates blanket is excessively "felted." When you squeeze a wool blanket the nap should spring back when you remove the pressure. Check the label for washing directions and degree of shrinkage before you buy.

Blankets too short? Relax. Just sew a strip of muslin to the end that is to be tucked in at the foot of the bed.

MATTRESSES

Happy dreams. We hope you don't toss and turn at night, but if you do, squeaking bedsprings won't bring on restful slumber. Instead of oiling the springs and thereby staining sheets, spray on liquid wax and out go the squeaks.

Oh, that aching back. It's often traceable to a lumpy mattress and can be avoided by turning mattress. Turn once a week for nonspring mattresses, every month for inner-spring mattresses. Keeps mattress from wearing unevenly and prolongs its usefulness. And you'll sleep better besides.

Handles on the mattress. If there are no loop handles on your mattress, sew on some sturdy strips of ticking. They're very helpful when it's time to turn the mattress.

Protect mattresses with sheet or mattress cover. Never roll a mattress; this is bad for innersprings and coverings. Place in special boxes made for this purpose.

BATHROOM

Cover wire towel hooks with corks to prevent holes from forming in towels when they hang for any length of time.

Double-duty mats. Make bath mats reversible, and use them twice as long, by sewing a Turkish towel on the reverse side.

Shower curtains last longer if soapy water is sponged off with clear water immediately after each use. Spread curtain out and allow it to dry before drawing it back.

Shower curtains stay put. Lightweight curtains don't hang properly and fly around when you're showering. Solve the problem by sewing weights (the kind used by dressmakers) in the bottom hem of the curtain.

MIRRORS

To make mirrors sparkling new. Wash them from a pan of water to which you've added one tablespoon of ammonia. Then dry and polish with tissue paper. They look beautiful.

To keep a mirror from fogging, apply film of soap with moistened finger, then polish the glass with soft cloth or cleansing tissue.

Scratchless mirrors. To protect the back of a mirror from scratches, cover it with a coat of clear shellac. Another reminder: the sun will cause mirrors to become cloudy. Hang them away from direct sunlight.

"Resilvering" mirrors. When a bare spot appears in your mirror, place a piece of smooth tinfoil over it on the back of the mirror. Paint over the tinfoil with shellac.

GLASSWARE

Life insurance for glassware. A glassmaker confides this nice little secret for strengthening glassware and making it less fragile: put it into a vessel filled with slightly salted water that you allow to come slowly to a boil. The slower the boiling, the hardier your glassware.

Glassware shock absorber. Place a silver spoon into any piece of good glassware or chinaware before pouring a hot liquid into it. Absorbs the shock of sudden sharp changes in temperature that may crack the glassware you prize.

Another tip. To avoid breakage, place ice cubes carefully into a glass; never drop them into an empty glass.

If one glass sticks to another, don't try to force them apart. Fill the glass on top with cold water, then dip the outer one in hot. They'll come apart without strain or breakage.

Prevent nicks in glassware. Handle and put glasses away carefully, so that edges do not bump together. Never stack. Store glasses with their rim sides up.

Save that nicked glass. When that hard-to-replace glass does get nicked, wrap a piece of "00" emery paper around the handle of a spoon and rub it back and forth across the nick until you've smoothed it down.

Washing delicate glassware. Glassware often cracks if put into hot water bottom first. Even very hot water will usually not hurt the most delicate glassware if you slip it in sideways or edgewise, slowly.

Give glassware extra sparkle by adding a few pinches of borax to the water when washing glassware.

Making jars and bottles smell fresh. Pour a solution of water and dry mustard into them, letting them stand for several hours; or use a diluted chlorine solution, then rinse in hot water.

Ammonia to the rescue. Use it in the water when washing greasy jars and bottles. Works like a charm.

To clean out the hard-to-remove sediment that often clings to the bottom of a bottle or glass vase, fill the vessel half full of warm soapsuds, add a handful of carpet tacks and shake vigorously.

To clean glass vases that have become stained, add some tea leaves to warm water and let it stand in the vase for several hours. Empty, then wash vase out with hot soapsuds and rinse in clear hot water. Another idea: soak in strong solution of hot vinegar, then wash in clear water. Either way the sparkle returns like magic.

To clean inside of glass drinking straws, run pipe cleaners through them.

CHINAWARE

How to tell real china from earthenware, often described as "china." Hold it up to the light. Earthenware is generally quite thick and porous in texture. China is nonporous and translucent. Through it you can see the light diffused.

Don't be afraid to use your good china. Instead of saving china dinnerware for special occasions, use it often, every day if you like. Its strength makes frequent use practical. Like your good silver, it grows lovelier with use.

China insurance. Never pour hot liquids into china cups just taken from a cold cupboard. First allow them to stand a short time at room temperature. Also, don't put fine china into the oven; the drastic temperature change may cause it to crack.

Care of china is simple. Because of its durability, it's simple to wash fine china. Use a mild dish-washing detergent, washing and rinsing with water as hot as your hands can stand. Avoid harsh detergents, gritty cleansers, and steel wool.

Most china can go into the dishwasher, except for china that can't be subjected to water as hot as is delivered to a dishwasher.

Stains on china. Clean off the stains but don't take off the decorations with them. Instead of scouring powder, which is hard on decorations, use salt and soda to cleanse away spots.

Keep your china clean. Wrap your best china in a plastic bag before putting it away, to keep it dust-free for the next use.

Cracked dishes. If the cracks are not too deep, you can probably make them invisible by boiling the dish in sweet milk for about an hour, over low heat. This is often a wonderful way to keep intact pieces that are hard to replace.

Save dish-washing time. Use your china in rotation, so that there's never a group at the bottom of the pile that remains unused for long. Always take dishes from the bottom of the pile. When washed and wiped, return them to the top. That way, none gathers dust.

After washing china, drain on a rubber mat or dish rack. Place the largest plates on the bottom when stacking them on the shelf. Store cups either on separate hooks or stacked by twos.

SILVERWARE

How to clean silver: Place silver in 1 gallon of hot water, using an aluminum pan. Add 1 tablespoon of ordinary salt and 1 teaspoon of soda. Then rinse and dry the silver.

Removing egg stains from silverware. Knives, forks, and spoons discolored by egg stains are easily cleaned by rubbing them with salt before washing, then rinsing in soapy water, followed by a clear-water rinse, and drying.

To prevent tarnishing, keep a piece of alum in the silverware drawer.

Rub furniture polish on silver vases and frames and notice how long it keeps them gleaming new and free of tarnish.

Simplest way to retard silver tarnish is to rinse thoroughly after washing. Even slight soap residue hastens tarnishing.

To clean tarnished silverware, place some boiling water in a large aluminum vessel and add 1 tablespoon of baking soda to each quart of water. Place the silver in this and let stand for about 15 minutes. Then rinse with hot water and dry. You'll be delighted with the results. Do not, however, use this method with "antiqued" silverware.

Tarnishproof silver storage. Wrap pieces of silver individually in tissue paper and store in tall potato-chip can. Seal cover with cellulose tape or store in airtight glass jars.

OTHER HOUSEHOLD METALS

Brassware needn't be hard to clean. Instead of polishing frequently, clean once, then apply a thin coat of fresh white shellac. Second coat gives still more protection. After this treatment, brass keeps clean with whisk of dustcloth.

Make your own brass polish. Here's how: Put 2 tablespoons salt into a cup of vinegar. Add just enough flour to form a smooth paste. Dip a damp cloth into the paste. Rub the brass until stains disappear. Rinse with cold water, then dry.

Tarnished brass. A lemon rind dipped in salt will remove most corrosion spots on brass.

To keep pewter brilliant, merely wash with hot suds, rinse, and dry. Silver polish will help.

Copper beautifier. Rub copper with salt and lemon juice or with salt and vinegar and you'll have it clean and sparkling richly in a jiffy.

Copper polish. Use the homemade polish given for brass on this page. But if green spots need removing, rub them with a cloth dipped in a weak solution of ammonia and water. Dry quickly, then polish with the paste mixture.

Keeps aluminum shiny. Aluminum will discolor if cleaned with harsh soaps or powders. Use a cloth moistened with lemon juice, rinse with clear water, dry thoroughly, and your aluminum will really brighten up.

Black's the wrong color for aluminum. If the inside of the aluminum pot starts turning black, slowly stew some acid food (rhubarb, tomatoes, etc.) and watch the sparkle return. The food won't be harmed.

Clean iron like magic A little vinegar and salt boiled in an iron skillet will remove untidy black spots or burns.

Iron pots and kettles won't rust if, after washing, you

wipe them thoroughly dry and then apply a little lard or other grease.

CARE FOR ODDS-AND-ENDS

To clean narrow-neck vases or bottles that have openings too small for a bottle brush, drop some crushed eggshells into the vessel, add a little water, and shake until all film and dust disappear from the glass. After rinsing, it will be crystal-clear.

Ashtray gum. Denatured alcohol does a miracle job of cleaning those black and gummy stains on ashtrays.

To clean plaster ornaments, try dipping them in thick liquid starch. Brush off the starch when dry and the dirt will come off with it, leaving the statuettes or ornaments spotless.

Keep those decorative candles clean with this jiffy treatment: rub them with a soft cloth dampened in a little alcohol.

Leather book covers need care, especially if not in constant use. When dusting, use a slightly oiled cloth occasionally, to restore some of the oil that has dried out of the leather.

Books stay new-looking if you clean soiled top edges, spread covers apart, grip the pages lightly, and rub gently with fine steel wool or sponge eraser.

When washing your lamp shades, prevent the colors from running by turning an electric fan on the shades as soon as you've rinsed them.

Parchment shades clean easily if you first coat them with a thin film of colorless shellac. Clean, when necessary, with a damp cloth.

25

Housecleaning

HOW TO KEEP YOUR HOME CLEAN WITH LESS WORK, LESS MONEY, LESS TIME

Housecleaning was once a major task that required a lot of physical exertion. Today, with all the special cleaning agents, much of the labor has been removed. Time is also saved—and, if you select properly, so is money. But you must inform yourself so as to know when it is wise to buy a specialized cleaning product and when it is more economical to buy some multi-purpose one.

A worker is only as good as the tools brought to the job, and this is true of housecleaning. With all the special tools and gadgets available, most of the hard labor can be eliminated. But as with cleaning agents, you must know which to buy and which not. Often some ordinary household item or little trick will do instead of an expensive appliance.

Scrub brush won't slip from your hand, and will be easier to use, if you fit a drawer knob into the wooden back. Also provides good grip for your hand.

Rack long-handled cleaning tools together. Brooms, mops, carpet sweepers, and even curtain rods should be slipped into spring clips high enough so they do not rest on the floor.

For worn-down sweepers. If the bristles on your carpet sweeper are beginning to wear short and won't pick up the dirt, try winding adhesive tape around the rollers, adhesive side down, facing the floor. This lets the brush down and the sweeper works better than ever. A cinch to do, too.

New mop out of old socks. Instead of discarding worn socks, clamp them into the holder and you've a fine new dry mop.

Sponge hint. Keep household sponges fresh by soaking them in cold salt water from time to time.

When chamois stiffens up, soak it in warm water to which a spoonful of olive oil has been added. Your chamois will emerge as soft and clean as when you bought it.

To move heavy furniture single-handed, lay an old rug or burlap sack on the floor close to it. Lift furniture onto rug, one end at a time. By pulling rug (or sack), furniture can be moved much more easily.

To clean under furniture that is too heavy to move easily, wrap a length of oil-treated cheesecloth to a flat stick (a yardstick will do very well) and slip this under the furniture, making sure that the end of the cloth-wrapped portion of the stick doesn't go all the way under. That keeps cloth from getting caught and remaining under the furniture.

HOW TO COPE WITH DUST AND DIRT

Your neighbors will love you if you don't shake dust mop out of the window. Lay it on the floor, on a piece of paper, then run the vacuum-cleaner nozzle over the top. Takes up dirt easily, quickly.

To collect the dust, dampen the inside of the dustpan and the broom bristle ends before sweeping. This will prevent dust from flying around. There's also a chemical you can spray on these convenient picker-uppers, as well as on dustcloths, which makes quick and dustless work of dusting. You can buy it in grocery and hardware stores.

Save time and work while dusting. Be sure to dust high objects first, so that any falling dust can be gathered later without your having to dust some things twice.

To keep dirt from accumulating in corners, shellac the baseboards in your room. Not only will this make sweeping far easier, but it will make cleaning the baseboards a relatively simple task of merely running a cloth over the surface from time to time.

Use a small syringe to suck out chips and dust when cleaning out a blind hole or crevice.

Dirt-proof that fireplace. Brick fireplaces that act as dirt catchers can be kept clean easily (and better-looking) if you brush the surface with liquid wax. Dust won't gather nearly as quickly and can easily be wiped off when it does.

Fireplace smoke stains. To clean the smoked areas on brick or stone, cover with a paste made of concentrated ammonia and powdered pumice. Let paste remain on for about 2 hours. Scrub off with hot water and soap. Rinse with clear water and dry.

WAYS TO LIVE BETWEEN CLEAN WALLS

Homemade solution for cleaning painted walls can be conjured up by combining 2 ounces of borax, 1 teaspoon of ammonia, and 2 quarts of water. You'll need no soap. Apply with a soft cloth.

Make wallpaper washable. Go over it first with sizing, then with a clear shellac. A damp cloth will clean it easily thereafter.

When cleaning washable wallpaper, make heavy suds, using warm water and mild soap, and apply with clean cloth. Don't let suds remain on the paper too long.

Protect wallpaper. Hold a cardboard against the wallpaper to prevent staining when you are painting or washing the woodwork.

Grease spots on wallpaper. Make a paste of cornstarch and water, let it remain on the spot until dry, then brush off. Usually works like magic. If it doesn't, try a paste of fuller's earth and grease solvent and use it the same way.

Wallpaper stained? Try these tricks:

Ink spots. Touch lightly with water and apply blotter, then treat with oxalic acid. If color of paper is affected, touch up with water colors or crayon.

Smudges. Work art gum eraser lightly over area. (Heavy rubbing may damage pattern of paper.)

Finger marks. Dampen with cold water and dust on a little powdered pipe clay or fuller's earth. After a few minutes remove with a soft brush.

Grease spots. Apply blotter over spot and hold it in place with a moderately hot iron. Finish cleansing with pipe clay or fuller's earth, as for finger marks.

Trick for the switch. The space around light switches sees a lot of traffic and, therefore, may be smudged frequently. After the space is cleaned, a thin coat or two of fresh white shellac will make the area around the switch easier to clean. An occasional quick dab with a damp cloth will then keep the space clean.

CARING FOR WOODWORK

To repair deeply scratched woodwork, fill scratches with mixture of fine sawdust and spar varnish. After filler has hardened completely, smooth down with fine sandpaper.

New surface. Small splits or "checks" that sometimes appear in old or weathered piece of plywood can be cleaned up with floor filler. Rub the filler into the cracks with burlap, working across the grain. When the material is dry and sanded, you'll have a smooth, solid base for a new paint coat.

"Starch" your woodwork. To remove smoke and grease stains, paint woodwork with a solution of starch and water. After the solution has dried, rub it off with a soft brush or clean cloth. This also removes the stains. Woodwork treated in this way doesn't harm the paint and stays good-looking for a very long time.

Kitchen-cabinet preservation. A coat of shellac on the interior of wooden kitchen cabinets not only provides protection from the steam and moisture always present in the kitchen, but keeps the wood surfaces of the cabinets from deteriorating. The shellac can be applied either before or after painting, and will work against dry rot and fungus growths as well as against moisture.

Rubber bumper. A chair positioned so it bumps the wall soon leaves an ugly mark. One way out: cushion the contact spot on the chair with a rubber-headed tack. A white one is best because it won't mark the wall.

Save the walls by applying a coat of colorless nail polish to upholsterer's nailheads on back of chairs placed against wall.

WINDOWS AND VENETIAN BLINDS

Window-cleaning hint. After washing a window, dry it on the inside with a sideways motion and on the outside with an up-and-down motion. Then if any streaks remain to be removed, you'll know instantly whether they are on the inside or on the outside of the window by the way the streaks run.

Keep Jack Frost away. On cold days rub alcohol or salt water on the outside of your windows, then polish them with newspapers. Keeps windows defrosted.

Spotless ledges. Window sills can be cleaned with

practically no effort if you give them a coating of wax. The wax protects paint. Rain and dirt wipe off in a jiffy.

Beautiful Venetian blinds. To clean and polish slats, first wipe them with a damp, clean cloth, or wash if necessary. Allow to dry. Then put on an old cotton glove, dipping the tips into polishing wax and rubbing the polish into the slats between the fingers.

Chamois is excellent for cleaning Venetian blinds. Soak soft chamois in solution of household detergent and warm water. Wring nearly dry before using. Result: Fast, lint-free job.

Clean white tapes on Venetian blinds from time to time with white shoe polish. They'll always look bright and fresh.

When you clean Venetian blinds, keep a spring-type clothespin handy. If phone or doorbell rings while you're working, slip the pin on the slat you've been cleaning, so you'll know where to resume work.

WOODEN FLOORS

Floor surfaces wear better if you wash them very thoroughly before applying wax or shellac.

Oil treatment for varnished floors. Clean daily with broom covered with a flannel bag, or with floor mop or soft brush (bare broom bristles drag grit along surface, scratch it). Go over the floor occasionally with a cloth or mop moistened in warm, soapy water. The less water on varnish, the better. After using damp cloth, dry floor at once. Then go over it with oiled cloth or mop.

Clean painted floors with a soft brush, then go over them with a floor mop, either dry or dampened with floor oil. If necessary, occasionally wipe with a damp cloth, then with a clean, dry mop. Afterward rub with oiled cloth or floor mop.

Remove floor scratches by rubbing with fine steel wool dipped in floor wax.

Remove rubber heel marks by wiping the spots with kerosene, turpentine, or floor oil.

Fill holes in the floor with plastic wood or with wood putty, stained to match. If you mix the wood putty or the plastic wood with weldwood glue you'll get a harder patch.

Silence those floor squeaks by dusting talcum powder or dripping glue into the cracks. (Works like magic.) Shellac the floor when dry.

Your rocker won't scratch waxed floor if you line the rocker arcs with adhesive tape.

Oil is bad for waxed floors. It dissolves the wax. Keep the floor clean with soft brush, dry floor mop, or floor-dusting attachment of your vacuum cleaner. When more thorough cleansing is needed, go over the floor with cloth wrung out of warm suds or one moistened, but not saturated, with turpentine. After every cleaning polish with weighted floor brush or polisher or rub briskly with soft cloth pad.

LINOLEUM

How to clean linoleum. Never flood linoleum surface with water. Use only wax on linoleum, never shellac, varnish, or lacquer.

Inlaid linoleum should be waxed, since varnish would tend to crack where breaks occur between inlaid pattern segments. Liquid wax is preferable to paste type, because it's easier to apply. Apply thin coat. Too much doesn't dry hard and simply becomes gummy.

Protect printed linoleum floor covering with coat of varnish. Some stores have special linoleum varnish; if this isn't available, use thin-bodied, light-colored floor varnish. Must be light or colorless to avoid staining light colors in the print.

To seal linoleum seams, run a strip of cellophane tape down the full length of the crack. Shellac over the tape and the surface will hold up indefinitely. The shellac coat will not only prevent dirt from seeping through but will also prevent tripping.

Loose linoleum edges look terrible and are a safety hazard, but they're easy to fix. Get some linoleum cement at the hardware store and work it under the loosened edge or corner, using a dull knife. Put an iron or a few heavy books over the area for at least 24 hours, until cement has hardened.

FINISHING TOUCHES

Got those ring-around-the-bathtub blues? Add a few drops of kerosene to the suds and watch those telltale markers disappear like magic.

Air purifier. Replace hospital smell of antiseptic cleansers with fresh, perfumed fragrance by pouring a little cologne into a saucer and lighting it. Heating the cologne first makes it burn better.

Are your cellar steps grimy? A little kerosene in the wash water will whiten them.

Discarded auto license plates make fine backstep scrapers. Your kitchen floor remains cleaner if muddy shoe soles are scraped out-of-doors. Nail old license plate to a corner of back doorstep.

26

Rugs and Carpets

HINTS ON INCREASING THE BEAUTY AND LIFE OF RUGS AND CARPETS—AND DIRECTIONS FOR REMOVING THE MOST COMMON STAINS

Unless otherwise mentioned, the following hints generally apply to cotton and synthetic (artificial) fiber floor coverings as well as to wool.

Three "beauty hints" for floor coverings. For long life and beauty, practice the three rules of rug care recommended by the National Institute of Rug Cleaning:

1. Clean daily with a carpet sweeper or vacuum cleaner. The carpet sweeper is a handy tool and is especially good for frequent light pick-ups. Light vacuuming is equally recommendable.

2. Carefully vacuum your rugs once or twice a week.

3. Have your rugs professionally cleaned at least once a year.

Cleanliness is the best defense against moth damage. You can effectively discourage moth larvae from feeding on your rugs and carpets by daily vacuuming and by using the professional rug cleaner's services at least once a year. If, for some reason, less frequent use of this professional service is necessary, apply one of the better known moth-repellent sprays around all the edges of the carpet and under all pieces of furniture three or four times a year. Food stains and other fatty or greasy substances should be removed as soon as seen. Under no circumstances roll up a rug and place it in attic, cellar, or storage room without first having it thoroughly cleaned.

CLEANING RUGS

Remove the "cutting edge" from your rugs and carpets. Dirt is the accumulation of heavy soil particles and sooty deposits that either stick to the surface of the rug pile or work their way deep down into it. Under constant footsteps, these sharp-edged particles cut rug fibers like hundreds of tiny knives, thus shortening rug life. They cannot be vacuumed away. The grease in this dirt is often as high as ten per cent, causing particles to cling tenaciously to pile fibers. Your best defense against this enemy is the use of good professional cleaning at least once a year.

If you decide to clean your rugs or carpets yourself, be careful about your choice of cleaning preparations. Read the directions and warnings on the labels before purchasing and make sure the particular substance is designed for the type of material your rug or carpet is made of. Some of the substances sold are not easily removed from the floor covering after they have been applied. The residue that remains in the rug will cause rapid resoiling and may damage colors or even the fabric. It may also trap dust particles and check their removal by vacuuming.

Go slow in using ammonia or preparations containing ammonia on your floor coverings, or soaps containing alkalies, such as heavy laundry soaps, strong dishwashing and floor-scrubbing compounds, and wall or sink cleaners. The pile of your rug and the dyes with which it has been colored may be sensitive to alkaline solutions; their use may cause discoloration or bleeding of colors, may even damage fibers.

Unless you really intend to shampoo your rugs regularly, you will probably not find it worthwhile to buy a shampoo machine. Especially as it is now possible to rent one at many outlets, including some supermarkets or hardware stores. By saving all your rug cleaning for one session, you can rent a shampooer for a short time and avoid the outlay, upkeep, and storage of owning a machine.

Shampoo your rug. Pick a day when the rug will dry quickly. Good ventilation and an electric fan will speed drying process. Proceed as follows: First vacuum the rug well on both sides. Place newspapers under rug edges to protect the floor. Test a small portion of the rug for colorfastness. Wash foot-square section at a time, being sure to overlap edges when going on to next section. Apply suds with flat, soft-bristled scrubbing brush, using a minimum of water. Rinse with damp (not wet) cloth. Never wet through to the back. Wait until it's all dry before replacing the furniture or walking on the rug.

TIPS ON RUG CARE

Turn your rugs around to face in different directions once or twice a year. This helps to distribute the wear over their entire surface.

Dents on carpeting can be fluffed back to shape by covering such spots with damp cloth, then applying hot iron and brushing with a stiff brush.

Keep stair rugs handsome. Make a point of shifting the front edges of stair rugs from time to time, since they receive the greatest wear.

To prevent rugs from slipping on hardwood floors,

glue or sew rubber jar rings to each corner. The suction will keep the rugs in place.

Let your professional rug cleaner rebind worn edges of rugs and carpets. Amateur attempts to trim off such edges only result in greater unraveling.

Clip the little tufts or "sprouts" that protrude above the surface of your floor covering with a pair of shears, but don't—no, *don't* pull them out.

Don't let shadows fool you. Most rugs and carpets, as well as other pile fabrics, don't stand up straight. Instead they have a natural slope in one direction known as the "lay" of the pile. Because of pile lay, almost all floor coverings, plain-colored ones in particular, show "shading," or light and dark areas. This is not a defect, but a common characteristic, and results simply from differences in reflections of light between the pile in its smooth normal condition and in its "ruffled" or irregular condition. If for any reason you are bothered by such shading, you can retard it to some extent by always finishing off each session of vacuuming by running your cleaner with the pile lay.

REMOVING STAINS

In case of accident. The following describes steps you can take to remove or check stains when they occur, using common household products from your kitchen cabinet or medicine chest. The methods described here are not those of the professional rug cleaner, who uses specialized stain-removal technique based on textile chemistry; they are emergency methods that you, as a homemaker, can apply when the inevitable spill takes place.

Treat stains while still fresh or wet. Unfortunately some stains can be effectively treated only with specialized skill and knowledge, while inexperienced attempts at removal can result in permanent damage. Therefore, while the emergency treatments suggested in the fol-

lowing pages may not always produce the desired results, they at least will not contribute to making a stain
permanent. In other words, by following these suggestions you can be confident of not doing the wrong
thing.

Caution. Several of the treatments suggested in the
following pages call for the use of nonflammable, home
dry-cleaning solvents that may be applied by sponging
or with a spray-type product. Many tufted rugs are
manufactured with rubber backing, and solvent applications should be light to prevent any possible damage
to the rubber. Paper (fiber) rugs are easily damaged
by spot-removal techniques. Mechanical action, especially when fiber is wet, must be kept to a minimum.

The "how" of emergency stain removal. First of all,
don rubber gloves to protect your hands from acquir-
ing the stain. Then arm yourself with one or more
pieces of clean, white, unstarched cloth, white absorbent tissue, or white paper towels. "Sponge out" as
much of the spill as possible with these. If you can,
place an old bath towel or uncolored cloth under the
stained area.

Always begin the first-aid operation at the outer
edges of the stained area and gradually work in from
the edges toward the center. If you work from the center out, you may enlarge the area of stain. Don't at any
time brush or rub stained area vigorously, as this action tends to distort the pile; even if the stain is removed, the disturbed pile may be more objectionable
than the stain. If a stain will respond to treatment at
all, it will respond readily without harsh rubbing.
Whenever possible, apply the solution recommended
for removal of the stain with a medicine dropper, and
apply it directly to the stain, not to the area outside the
stain.

Quick formulas for stain removal. With one of these
formulas, or, where indicated, the right combination of

formulas, you can proceed to tackle a variety of common stains resulting from accidents. If a mishap occurs, refer to the specific cause of the stain in the following list. It indicates the formula to use and how to use it.

Formula 1. Put a teaspoonful of detergent in a jar, mixing bowl, or other container. Add a cup of water and stir vigorously until you have a clear solution with no residue. (The amount of suds has no bearing on the effectiveness of the formula.) Apply this solution, where recommended, directly on the stain with an eye dropper. Using a rotary motion, sponge the stained area with a clean, white, unstarched cloth, beginning at the outer edge and working in. Try to keep inside the stained area at all times. Blot up remaining moisture with damp cloths, sponging in the direction of the pile lay. Finally, with another cloth dampened in clean, lukewarm water, sponge the area again several times. Finish by blotting up remaining moisture with damp cloths.

Formula 2. Mix a teaspoonful of white vinegar with 2 teaspoonfuls of lukewarm water. Apply this solution directly to the stained area with a medicine dropper. Using a rotary motion, gently agitate the saturated area with a clean, white, unstarched cloth. Allow the solution to remain on the stain for about 15 minutes. Blot up remaining moisture with damp cloths. With another cloth dampened in clean, lukewarm water, sponge the area again several times. Finish by sponging in the direction of the pile, blotting up remaining moisture with damp cloths.

SPECIFIC STAINS

Animal urine. In homes with pets, floor-covering accidents are not only the most common but the most serious. As stated previously, the fibers and dyes in woolpile floor coverings are sensitive to strong alkaline

solutions. And when the moisture content of the urine evaporates, a highly concentrated alkaline deposit remains. This alkaline concentration then reacts to cause an actual change of color. However, when animal stains are properly treated as soon as they occur, color change can be held to a minimum.

Treatment. Sponge the stained areas with several applications of clean lukewarm water. Use a damp, clean, unstarched cloth or cellulose sponge to absorb as much of the moisture as possible. Apply Formula 2 as directed. Allow to dry thoroughly and apply Formula 1. Allow to dry thoroughly. Apply Formula 2 again, as directed. This treatment is effective in a great percentage of cases. Where a color change actually takes place, however, no further treatment can restore the color. Your professional rug cleaner, nevertheless, can have the rug redyed if it is a solid color rug. Or if it is a pattern rug, he may be able to improve its appearance by spot-dyeing the affected areas.

Beverages—alcohol, coffee, tea, soft drinks. Sponge the area with lukewarm water, using clean, white unstarched cloth or cellulose sponge. Absorb and repeat several times. Follow with Formula 1 as directed. If necessary, follow with Formula 2. Most beverages contain a certain kind of sugar that is colorless when first deposited on a fabric. After it has been exposed to air for some time, however, this invisible sugar stain undergoes a chemical change called caramelization and it sets permanently in the rug fibers. Later on, after exposure to direct sunlight or heat used for drying cleaned rugs, the stain may appear as a delayed-action tan or brown discoloration. Consequently, treat such spills immediately.

Blood. Sponge with cool water. Follow with Formula 1. If a yellowish stain results, apply a few drops of peroxide. Allow to remain 2 or 3 minutes. Follow by sponging with clear, cool water.

Butter and fats. Apply any nonflammable household dry-cleaning fluid to the stain with an eye dropper and sponge with a clean, white, unstarched cloth. Observe "Caution," page 207.

Cosmetics. Apply a nonflammable household dry-cleaning fluid, then follow with Formula 1 as directed. Observe "Caution," page 207.

Egg, gelatin, mucilage. Apply Formula 1 as directed. If stain remains, apply Formula 2 as directed.

Foodstuffs, general. If it's a "crusty" food, gently scrape off as much as possible with a dull knife or spatula. Follow by sponging with lukewarm water, using a clean, white, unstarched cloth, then apply Formula 1. If any trace of stain remains after area dries, apply a nonflammable househould dry-cleaning fluid with an eye dropper and sponge dry with a clean cloth. Observe "Caution," page 207.

Fruits and fruit juices. Sponge with a clean white cloth dampened with lukewarm water. Follow with Formula 1.

Furniture polish. Removal of furniture polish is one of the more difficult stain-removal tasks. Very often these stains are insoluble because the polish contains a dye that has an affinity for the fibers of the rug and the chemical action necessary to remove the stain may often remove the color of the rug as well. Apply a nonflammable household dry-cleaning fluid, and sponge with a clean cloth. If this is ineffective, allow the solvent to evaporate and apply Formula 1 as directed. Observe "Caution," page 207.

Furniture stains. Spots from wood dyes and stains from bottoms of chair and table legs sometimes occur. These are often difficult or impossible to remove. Consult your professional rug cleaner.

Grease. Apply a nonflammable dry-cleaning fluid and sponge with a clean cloth. Repeat until the cloth shows no further evidence of discoloration. Observe

"Caution," page 207. If any strain remains, apply Formula 1.

Ice cream, milk, desserts. Sponge with lukewarm water, using a clean, white, unstarched cloth. Follow with Formula 1.

Ink (ball-point pen). Apply a nonflammable household dry-cleaning fluid, and sponge with a clean, dry cloth. Observe "Caution," page 207.

Ink (other than ball-point). Ink stains are another common source of trouble to the homemaker. Since there are many kinds of inks, there have been hundreds of formulas suggested for ink removal. While many of them produce satisfactory results, their misuse often causes a small stain to spread over a larger area of the floor covering. Nearly all household inks, except ball-point pen inks (see page 174), are soluble in soap and water. However, excessive use of soap and water will extend the stain over too large an area of the carpet for an inexperienced person to tackle. Where the stain or stains are small, do this:

Use clean white tissues to blot up as much of the stain as possible. Have an abundance of these or clean white rags available and be sure to don your rubber gloves. Sponge the stain from its outer edges in toward the center. Repeat the spongings as long as you can see evidence of the stain on the cloths you are using. Follow by using Formula 1, again being careful to work in toward the center of the stain. Changing cloths frequently, repeat until all evidence of the stain is removed. Don't use milk.

If a brown or yellow stain remains, this is evidence that iron was incorporated in the ink formula. Its removal is a job for your rug cleaner.

Removing large ink stains can be a very messy chore. It is best to merely blot up as much ink as you can, then call your professional rug cleaner. Permanent-ink stains, however, usually can't be removed.

Iodine. Apply a few drops of white vinegar to stain. Mix a solution, using 1 teaspoon of hypo crystals (obtainable from drug or photography-supply store) in a glass of warm water. Apply with an eye dropper, a drop or two at a time, and carefully sponge with a clean white cloth from the outside to the center. Repeat as often as necessary. Follow by sponging with clean lukewarm water. Blot up remaining moisture with damp cloths.

Medicine (general). Sponge with lukewarm water and clean, white, unstarched cloths, changing cloths as often as necessary and working from the outer edge toward the center. Apply one drop of Formula 1 to the stain and immediately apply a cloth to that area. If there is evidence of the stain transferring to the cloth, continue with Formula 1. If not, follow the same procedure with Formula 2. If the stain still doesn't respond, find out from your physician or druggist the chemical content of the medicine. Then call your professional rug cleaner and pass on to him the information as to chemical content. With this information he can determine the best way to remove the stain.

Nail polish, household cement, dope. Nail polish, household cement, or airplane dope may damage a rug or carpet made of synthetic fibers or blends. Home treatment of these stains with agents such as nail-polish remover or thinner may also be very damaging. Apply chemically pure amyl acetate directly to the stain with an eye dropper. After a few minutes sponge with a clean, white, unstarched cloth, working from the outer edge in toward the center.

Oil. Most oil stains will respond to the use of a nonflammable household dry-cleaning fluid, applied by eye dropper to the stained area and sponged with a clean, white, unstarched cloth. Where such stains cover a large area and are caused by an appreciable amount of oil, the cost of attempting to remove them in the

home is prohibitive. Send the rug to your professional rug cleaner or call him into your home. Observe "Caution," page 207.

Paint, varnish, shellac. Where a small quantity of such material has been dropped on the rug, apply turpentine with an eye dropper and sponge it from the outer edge of the stain toward the center. Follow by applying a nonflammable dry-cleaning fluid in the same manner. If the stain remains, contact the paint manufacturer for a thinner or remover made especially for the product involved. Where the stains are caused by considerable spillage, the cost of home removal makes the effort impractical. Better let your professional rug cleaner remove the stain. Observe "Caution," page 207.

Rust. Removal is no job for an amateur. Better call your professional rug cleaner.

Shoe polish, liquid. If the stains are in small local areas in the floor covering, apply a nonflammable dry-cleaning fluid with an eye dropper and sponge the area from the outer edge in toward the center of the stain. Repeat as often as necessary and while there is evidence that the stain is being transferred to the cloth. Observe "Caution," page 207. If not entirely successful, apply Formula 1, as directed.

Shoe polish, paste. Scrape off any crusty surface, using a dull knife or spatula. Apply a nonflammable dry-cleaning fluid with an eye dropper, sponging from the outer edge toward the center of the stain. Repeat as often as necessary and while there is evidence that the stain is being transferred to the cloth. Observe "Caution," page 207. If not entirely successful, apply Formula 1.

Sugar stains (candy, chocolate, syrup, etc.). Scrape off any crusty surface with a dull knife or spatula. Sponge with lukewarm water, working from the outer edge of the stain toward the center. Follow with Formula 1 as directed.

Wax. Scrape off as much as possible with a dull knife or spatula. Apply a nonflammable dry-cleaning fluid and sponge with a clean cloth. Observe "Caution," page 207.

Stains of unknown origin. Any attempt to remove a stain of unknown origin with a patent cleaning preparation may set the stain and make it impossible for even your professional rug cleaner to remove. If you insist on attempting the removal of a "mystery" stain, it is wise to confine your activity to the following:

Apply a nonflammable household dry-cleaning fluid with an eye dropper and sponge with a clean, white, unstarched cloth, working from the outer edge toward the center. Observe "Caution," page 207. If the cloth picks up some of the stain, repeat the application until either the stain is removed or there is no further transfer to the cloth. Follow with Formula 1. If still unsuccessful, phone your rug cleaner.

27

Household Handyman

A MISCELLANY OF HELPFUL TIPS FOR ALL THOSE LITTLE THINGS THAT NEED DOING

Don't waste shoe polish. To get the polish that clings to sides of tin after center part has been used, hold tin over low heat. The wax will melt and form new cake of polish.

Did you ever think of a bottle cap as an umbrella tip? It's really quite an idea. Plastic bottle tops (from cologne, nail polish, etc.) are colorful and practical replacements for lost umbrella tips. Fasten in place with household cement.

For wet umbrellas. A large sponge placed in the bottom of your umbrella stand will absorb the dripping water.

Newspaper rug pad. If you haven't a regular rug pad, use newspapers under your large rugs. Spread several layers flat under the rugs and you'll save wear, make the rugs look and feel better underfoot, make the floor warmer, provide a soft, luxurious tread.

Thumbtacks prevent dust marks. Place one thumbtack in each lower corner at the back of a picture frame and the tack heads will provide air space between picture and wall, thus preventing dust line from soiling the wall surface.

A fair deal with cards. If playing cards stick together, rub some talcum powder over them and you'll have a smooth new deal.

Precondition your new toothbrush by soaking it in cold water for 24 hours before using. This preserves the bristles for a longer time.

Fireplace magic transforms kindling wood into logs. With one or two nails, fasten together several pieces of wood otherwise useful only as kindling. They'll become as long-burning as a regular log.

A colorful touch for your open fire. Soak pine cones in chemical solution and add to your firewood. Dry cones thoroughly after soaking, before you burn them. Copper nitrate produces emerald green, potassium nitrate gives you orange, lithium, chloride gives a purple glow.

MINOR MENDS AND REPAIRS ABOUT THE HOUSE

Remove broken light bulb safely. Press a large cork into the base of the bulb and unscrew it easily without having to touch the jagged edges of the bulb.

Extracting key if broken. If you break off a key in a lock, run an old jigsaw blade into the cylinder alongside the broken piece and twist it so that the teeth bite into the key. Pulling on the blade while in this position usually will remove the broken piece.

Outwit the lid. Those frustrating struggles with a jar lid that won't come loose can be eliminated by lining your hand with sandpaper before turning. You'll be able to grip like mad.

Glue lid opens easily. After opening a new bottle of glue, rub a little lard or oil on the bottle top before putting back the lid. It will come off quickly the next time you want to open it.

Mend breaks in your toothpaste tube (or any other kind of tube) with a strip of sturdy Scotch tape wrapped twice around the tube. Saves you money keeps tube neat.

Use modeling clay, in mending chinaware or glass, to hold chipped pieces together while the mending cement is hardening.

To remove dents from pots, pans, trays, place dented surface against firm, level object (upturned flatiron often works), with bumpy surface facing you. Using medium-heavy hammer, tap the protruding dent with slow, light raps (heavy hammer blows will mark up the surface around the dent). A dozen blows or so will turn the trick.

Hot-water bag mended fast. If the hot-water bag springs a leak, tamp adhesive tape down over the tear. For a permanent mend, however, apply an inner-tube patch (same as is used on tire tubes).

Emergency home shoe repairing. Run-down rubber heels, cuts, and other worn spots can be built up with rubber-base tire-cut filler, available in tube containers. Spread over worn area, allow to dry overnight. This material is self-adhering and self-vulcanizing.

Tape keeps plaster from chipping. When driving a nail into a plaster surface there's always danger of chipping. Before you start stick a bit of Scotch tape over spot where nail is to be driven in and you are more likely to prevent the chips from flying.

Rag rugs stay put. Those little rag rugs are attractive but are such a nuisance when they curl. Dipping the ends in weak starch after they have been washed will keep them on the straightaway.

Sticking metal to wood. First soak the metal in acetone. When dry, use household cement to attach it to the wood. Don't touch the cleaned area of the metal before cementing.

Repair holes or short tears in canvas by using rubber cement to apply the patching material. Weight the patch for several hours to be sure it will stay in place.

FABRIC CARE

Permanent-wave solutions. Usually stains from these do not show up immediately upon contact. It may take days, weeks, before they do. So, when having a home permanent, protect garment completely. Not even your dry cleaner can guarantee removal results.

White furs that have yellowed. Many white furs are originally bleached with a "reducing bleach." After a time they take on oxygen from the air and start turning yellow. This can be overcome, usually, by spraying on a solution of hydrogen peroxide or by brushing with a soft brush. Sometimes hanging fur in the sun afterward will speed up the rebleach job.

"Pilling" of fabric. Surface yarns (as in bouclés and poodle cloth) sometimes roll themselves up into a small accumulated ball (sometimes happens with smooth-surface fabrics too). Brush with coarse, dry brush. If you're very careful, you may be able to remove the pilling by stretching fabric tight and "shaving" surface with safety razor. But take care not to cut the cloth itself.

Suède glove freshener. Put gloves on and rub hand with thick slice of stale bread, changing to another slice as bread becomes soiled.

If careless you, or one of your guests, burned a cigarette hole in your lovely bridge cloth, don't be dismayed. Cover that hole with an appliquéd design or monogram, of a contrasting color, using thread to match the appliqué. Or if the hole is minute, embroider a little design or monogram over it with same or contrasting thread.

If party guests leave coats on your bed, protect both spread and wraps by covering spread with sheet of pliofilm or plastic tablecloth. Keeps coats from picking up lint, protects spread from soiling.

PERSONAL COMFORT

Tired feet mean a tired you. Two handfuls of ordinary salt in a basin of hot water give you new feet for old. Epsom salts, bicarbonate of soda, or ordinary brown laundry soap make a mighty refreshing foot bath too.

Clean eyeglasses. Opticians recommend an occasional soap-and-water bath for your glasses to remove the film of oil that gathers from the skin. Rinse, then polish with soft tissue paper.

When particles of adhesive stick to your skin after removing bandage, rub with acetone and rinse with water. Use absorbent cotton to apply acetone.

Smoke disperser. Soak a towel in water, swish it around the room, and watch how quickly smoke disappears. Another idea: dispel smoke and other odors by leaving a saucer of vinegar in the room.

Soundproofing the sickroom. Cover watch or small clock on bedside table with large glass tumbler. Patient can see the time when wanted, but won't be disturbed by sound. Muffle telephone bell with thick cloth covering.

Keep phone easy to reach. Have telephone connected in spot that saves the most steps. If house has two floors, place phone on stair landing rather than remote room on either floor, if you can't afford the luxury of an extension phone.

MODERN APPLIANCES NEED LITTLE CARE

Manufacturers are your friends. When you buy household appliances don't throw out the descriptive booklets provided by the manufacturers. They'll give you helpful hints on the "ounce of prevention" that will keep the appliance in shape for maximum time. Keep instruction booklets in handy drawer or kitchen file and refer to them until you are completely acquainted with your new appliances.

They're longer-lasting than you think. Many household appliances appear to have outlived their usefulness before they really have. If toaster, cleaner, washer, or other appliance gives you much trouble, don't immediately discard it for a new one. Instead consult your dealer and see if replacement of some parts can make the appliance as good as new again.

They run themselves these days. All you have to do is turn on the switch and your appliance takes over your work for you. Because this automaton requires intricate mechanism to operate, however, don't try for home repairs if something goes wrong. Any large manufacturer, and they are numerous, has factory-trained and skilled repair men who will save you money and lengthen the life of your appliance if you call them in at the first sign of faulty operation. Simply consult the classified section of your telephone directory to find the right repair service.

If any automatic appliance becomes noisy, it's time to call a service man. In fact, you can often prevent trouble from threatening or developing if you have an arrangement with your service man to check all your home appliances once a year.

EFFICIENT LIGHTING

Get in the habit of turning off lights when you leave a room and are not planning to return to it for a while.

Cut down on light bulbs by using one high-wattage one instead of several smaller bulbs. A 100-watt bulb gives 50 per cent more light than four 25-watt ones yet costs only a few pennies more per bulb than the small size.

Don't skip the bulbs when you're dusting. Few homemakers realize that a few swipes with a cloth over a dusty light bulb can increase light by as much as 50 per cent. Be sure lamp shades are dusted on the inside as well as outside.

Colored bulbs, except the pale pink ones you use for atmosphere rather than for illumination, serve no good purpose. They greatly lessen the bulb's potential light yield.

Best light from table lamp is assured if the base is at least 12 inches high.

Check your lamp shades. Solid dark shades and dark shade linings reflect less light than light transparent ones. You'll see better with the light shades and room has a cozier look.

Wall-reflected light is free. When you repaint, use white or light pastel shades. Rooms so painted require far less artificial lighting than those with dark walls.

Basement walls painted a light color or whitewashed reflect more light than dark walls. If overhead joists are exposed, you'll increase amount of illumination from ceiling fixture without using a higher-watt bulb this way: Nail to the joist several painted white boards or piece of plywood on white cardboard.

AT THE DESK

A note about inks. Permanent inks are for documents meant to last a long time and withstand possible exposure to water or strong light; if spilled, chances are they can't be removed without fabric injury.

Washable ink is for general use. If spilled on color-fast material, soak up as much as possible with blotter. (See stain-removal chapter for specific instructions.)

Inkstains on fingers. To remove them moisten the stain, then rub with the sulphur end of a match and wipe with a dry cloth.

When you open a new box of stationery, paste a small envelope inside the cover. Use it to hold stamps and air-mail stickers and you'll have them handy as needed.

When adhesive on envelope flap doesn't stick, try quick application of nail polish. Dries quickly, leaves no smudge. Can't even be steamed open.

Novel key ring at very low cost, especially valuable to people who have to remove keys from ring frequently, is a simple metal shower-curtain hook.

Paper clip does double duty as a pencil clip. Straighten out one end and wrap it around pencil.

Make your own rubber bands. When you discover holes in your rubber gloves, convert them into rubber bands instead of throwing them out. With a pair of scissors cut across the width of each finger, the palm, and the wrist. You'll have quite a few first-class rubber bands of different sizes, cut just the thickness you want.

STORING TIPS

What's in it? Label each package before you put things away in your attic, basement, or extra closet. This will save you needless unwrapping, bewilderment, and time when you finally do want some of the contents. Sounds obvious, but the reminder seems needed.

Speed up packing job. Packing cardboard cartons goes faster if flaps are held open by small sections of garden hose, split apart on one side to form rubber clamps. Saves your temper as well as your time.

To tie tight, secure package, use wet string. It shrinks as it dries and thus gets tighter.

Heat sealing. Cellophane or pliofilm wrappings may be heat-sealed with a warm hand iron, curling iron, or specially made electric heater sealer. Don't apply the heating tool directly to the pliofilm, but iron through cellophane so pliofilm won't melt or stick to your iron.

Shelf paper won't tear as quickly if you secure it with transparent adhesive instead of thumbtacks.

Save egg cartons for Christmas time. They make excellent containers in which to store your colorful tree ornaments.

Newspapers have many uses, even after the family has finished reading them. Save for packing clothes out of season or rolling in rugs put up for the summer. Newsprint also discourages moths. A well-crumpled newspaper is also handy for wiping windows dry, leaves no linty coating.

Store garden shoes and rubbers in the garage. Off in a free corner, hammer several large nails into the wall. Use these as pegs for the footwear. Keeps them in shape; they gather less dust, too.

Before storing overshoes, wash outside surface with warm water to remove oil and grease spots as well as encrusted dirt. Stuff with crumpled newspaper and store in dark, cool, dry place.

Use sandwich bags for wool storage. Small items— balls of yarn, mittens, etc.—can be mothproofed for storage by placing them in plastic bags together with some mothballs or moth flakes. Seal the open end of the bag with adhesive or some kind of tape.

To store tennis racquets for the winter, cover them first with a coating of petroleum jelly. Prevents strings from snapping when not in use.

It's easy to slide heavy storage boxes if you tack four or more metal bottle caps to the base of the box. Caps raise the box and reduce friction between it and the floor. Saves "elbow grease," costs you nothing.

A stored card table won't flop on its side if kept in place with a homemade cleat. An inexpensive towel bar, fastened to the wall on a diagonal line, serves beautifully.

MOVING AIDS

Shred old newspapers as packing filler for bric-a-brac, dishes, stemware, and even lamp shades. Pack each shade separately after first wrapping in tissue paper.

Packing liquid preparations for travel. Bind corks or stoppers with adhesive or Scotch tape before packing. This keeps the containers leakproof, prevents costly damage to clothes.

For safety and ease of handling, pack books on end and one row deep in strong cartons or boxes. If box is wide enough for two rows, pack with books back-to-back. Saves the bindings.

Dresser drawers won't rattle or break, when moved, if packed with lightweight things. Best idea is to double-fold pillows into the drawers.

Don't lose the screws. When you take down the curtain rods, towel racks, etc., for moving, fasten all the screws to them with pieces of Scotch tape. Then they'll be handy when you put the piece back in place.

28

The House

DIRECTIONS AND TIPS FOR CARE AND REPAIR OF THE BASIC FABRIC OF YOUR HOUSE

Proper maintenance of the basic fabric and fixtures of a house not only makes living there more pleasurable but keeps the house's value rising over the years, so that in financial terms, too, you get your investment back. Not everyone will be able to do all the major jobs over the lifetime of a house, but everyone can certainly undertake some of the simpler chores. Both types are explained here, from hints on tools to directions for electrical repairs.

TIPS ON TOOLS

Improvise a neat holder for small tools. Small files, pliers, screwdrivers, etc., can be held in place and carried around conveniently while you work if you rack them into the closely packed bristles of a scrubbing brush. The inverted brush back makes an excellent stand to keep them upright.

Hardware-storage tip. Store bolts, screw, washers, etc., in compartments of plastic ice-cube tray. Compartments are deep enough to prevent mixing of contents.

Keep cutting tools keen. To keep rust from forming on your chisels, bits, and similar tools, wrap them in an oil-soaked rag before putting them away. This wrapping will also keep the tools from being dulled or injured as a result of striking each other in a drawer.

Another anti-rust trick. Keep few cones of carpenter's blue chalk in toolbox to absorb moisture. Every two months dry chalk thoroughly in an oven to renew its effectiveness.

To clean a file, place a strip of adhesive tape lengthwise over it. Rub finger over tape, to press it firmly between file teeth. Then pull it off. Imbedded shavings, dust, etc., come off easily with tape.

Preserve hardware labels from mold that may form after several months. Coat labels with spar varnish when you buy supplies; then, no matter how long you have them, label will be easy to read. White shellac works too.

Handy holder for tape measures can be made from empty adhesive-tape spool. Use the spool cover to keep the tape measure free from dust.

Run your drill through the bottom of a cheese or ice-cream carton to catch the chips when you drill overhead holes.

Increase usefulness of old brushes with lacquer. By applying lacquer at the base of a brush you keep bristles from shedding.

Protect an outdoor padlock by nailing a rectangle of stiff leather on the door above the padlock. This little "roof" over the lock keeps ice or snow from dripping into the lock, where mechanism might rust or freeze in cold weather.

Make your flashlight see around corners. Clamp bicycle mirror to flashlight. Directs beam of light at angle and reflects article at which it is directed. A clever convenience when doing repair work on car or on plumbing installations.

No one to hold your flashlight? Improvise a holder with a funnel. Invert the funnel, slip a rubber band over its neck, then use the rubber band to hold the flashlight in place. You can slide the light backward and forward until it's just where you want it.

NAILS AND SCREWS

Soap to the rescue. Before driving a nail into wood, push it through a cake of hard soap. Nail will then go through wood without danger of splitting it.

To drive nails easily into hard wood, dip point of each nail in oil or hard grease beforehand.

Nails are the wrong answer when linoleum floor coverings starts to break near the doorway. Either make a clean cut, removing broken section and cementing new piece securely into place, or place a metal edge over the ragged part. (Nails only damage the linoleum.)

To remove headless nails that have been driven into hardwood, grip end of nail with pliers. Then use claw hammer to lift both pliers and nail.

When picture nails come loose from the plaster, all you need to get them back in place is a strip of cloth and some glue. Wrap narrow strip of cloth around shank of nail, dip into glue, and replace in the hole in the plaster. Allow glue to dry for 24 hours before replacing picture.

Screw won't give? Try this. Don't give up if you've tried with all your might to loosen a screw that refuses to turn. Try again with the heated edge of a screwdriver.

Screw loose? If a screw has worked loose in its hole, remove it, insert solid wire solder, and retighten.

Another way with loose screws. Insert wooden slivers or tamp wood putty into the old hole before replacing the screw.

To salvage screws with mangled heads, reslot head with hacksaw.

Steel wool, packed in screw hole, will also tighten loose screws.

WORKING WITH GLUE

A powerful homemade glue. If you've been having trouble finding a glue that will stick glass to glass, leather to metal, or other unusual combinations, burn some shellac in a dish to get rid of the alcohol. The remainder will be one of the strongest and best all-purpose glues you've ever used.

Prevent after-mess in gluing jobs. Place a piece of waxed paper on top of glued article before putting on weights, to help hold pieces together as glue hardens. Prevents weight from clinging to glued object.

"Combing in" the glue. To apply a thin coat of glue uniformly over a large surface, use a fine-tooth comb as a spreader. Especially handy when working on large pieces of veneer.

Soften up hardened glue by placing a few drops of vinegar in the container.

PLASTER WORK

To keep that crack from reopening when you patch plaster, first scrape the crack clean, then wet it thoroughly before you plaster. When dry, coat the patch with shellac.

Use two putty knives instead of one when you patch with plaster. By using one wide and one narrow knife, you can keep both clean and much easier to work with.

Slow that plaster down so that you don't have to race against its inclination to harden fast. How? Simply add a little sugar or vinegar when mixing.

Always add the plaster to the water. Don't ask why. You'll have trouble getting a good mix if you do it the other way around.

Patching a giant hole? Use a section of plasterboard

to fit the hole. You'll need less plaster and do a much better job.

Plaster wall turning to powder? Usual cause: the plaster was first applied in a dry, hot room so that it dried out before it could set. To mend this condition, try a gentle water spray with an insecticide gun.

Plaster holes disappear. Small nail or screw holes in a plastered wall are annoying. An easy way to fill them is to sharpen a piece of ordinary chalk to a point, then press the point into the hole and cut it off. Next sandpaper the chalk flush with the wall and coat it with fresh shellac. Match the wall color with a little paint.

Another plaster-saver. Heat the nail first before driving in. It will go in smoothly and won't take a chunk of plaster with it.

DOORS

Modernize that old door easily by gluing and screwing (or nailing) a plywood panel over it. You'll have to remove the paint from the door so the glue will hold tight. If you use paint remover, don't forget to wash afterward with alcohol. Use common ¼-inch plywood, or, if you wish, choose a ply with a handsome hardwood face.

So you're going to do it the easy way. Hang a door? Slip some pieces of wood of the correct thickness under your door when you stand it up to locate the hinge cutouts.

Doors drag? Try tightening the screws that hold the hinges in place. If they just won't tighten, fill the screw holes with plastic wood and try again when dry.

Cardboard solves problem of door that won't shut. If a door won't stay closed, this may be caused by shrinkage of the wood in the door. To eliminate this nuisance, unscrew hinges and place one or more thicknesses of cardboard behind leaf of hinge that is fastened to the doorframe. Then fasten hinges in place again.

Doors won't latch as easily as they should when there is an accumulation of paint or dirt in the doorframe corner, when the bolt is sticky and won't extend easily, or when the latch has been pushed back out of place.

A shot of graphite powder into the door lock at least once a year will keep it in fine operating condition for the life of the house. Pencil-point shavings will do the trick fine too.

If driving rain seeps in under one of your outside doors, you can stop the leakage by making a shallow saw cut in the lower edge of the door where it stands on the sill. When the water gets to this little crack it has a tendency to run back out-of-doors instead of coming on in. The saw cut, of course, must be on the outside edge of the door.

STAIRS

Creaky stairs are nearly always caused by loose treads. If you can conveniently get underneath the step, tighten the guilty wedges. If you can't, drive long finishing nails at an angle into the risers, through the treads. (Through the vertical sections, of course.)

To save the price of new stair treads, remove the worn ones carefully, turn them over, and renail. This is easy to do in almost all cases.

To banish nicked edges on stair treads, patch with one of the commercial brands of synthetic woods or make your own filler with glue and sawdust. If it is an especially large hole, drive a couple of nails beneath the surface to help hold the patch in place.

FLOORS

Don't expect new floors to lie perfectly flat. Even the best grade of flooring is usually slightly imperfect. Figure the cost of sanding the floor down as part of the normal cost of a new floor.

Before you invest in power-sanding your old floor, try washing it down with special, high-power floor soap. Use rubber gloves. In many cases the soap will restore the lightness and brightness of your dark floor.

Floors may be covered with a number of liquid applications but the most popular coating if you are interested in preserving the wood's natural grain and color is polyurethane. This synthetic resin varnish has generally replaced such traditional coatings as shellac. Polyurethane has several qualities that recommend it: durability, long life, waterlike clarity, good flexibility, and a fast drying time. The wood should be clean and free from any other substances as possible. (Never, in any case, apply wax to untreated wood for it will penetrate without protecting the surface.) Follow the directions on the can of polyurethane and you should end up with fine, natural wood floors.

Baseboard or wood trim warped? Try drilling a clearance hole through the board at its greatest bulge and running a flat-headed wood screw into the stud underneath. If you can't, pull the board up all the way, fill the space between the board and the wall with putty or plaster and paint.

Quick trim for damaged woodwork. It's not necessary to replace wood trim that has been damaged along the edges. Most times you can plane a new edge and repaint. Even though the repaired trim may be narrower and of different edge shape than its neighbors, the difference will be scarcely noticeable.

THE BATHROOM

To rewhiten blackened cracks between ceramic tiles, scrub clean with a stiff brush. Mix white tile cement and water to make a paste. Rub this paste into the soiled joints, but wipe the tile clean before putting on the paste. In this way you can renew an entire wall in just a few minutes.

Bathroom fixtures can be mounted quickly by using any of the many cements made for this purpose. It is no longer necessary to remove the old tile and bolt the fixture to the wall.

The seal between the tub and wall often crumbles away and leaves an unattractive open space. Make your own resealer out of white tile cement. Simply mix until it forms a paste and apply.

Ceramic tiles are easy to use, and you can get them in all sizes and colors. Use white tile cement to set. On wood surfaces first nail a wire screen into place (about ½ inch square), then apply cement and tile.

New tile sinks. When your tile sink becomes chipped, touch it up with a wax crayon in matching color, then coat with a transparent mending cement. This will stand up nicely under many washings and can easily be renewed.

Chipped porcelain-enamel sink or tub? Cover it with special enamel made for the purpose. It will still look somewhat patched, but looks much better white, in kitchen or bathroom, than black or rusty. You can find sink enamel at your hardware store.

BASIC PLUMBING REPAIRS

Only a drop in the bucket? A faucet that leaks one drop per second means a loss of 700 gallons of water a year. Check and repair immediately.

To stop that faucet drip, resurface the valve seat before you replace the washer. (This can be done with a handy tool that sells for a modest price at your hardware store.) Shut off the water. Take apart the faucet. Screw the tool into the faucet and turn a few times. (When replacing, be sure to use red washers for the hot water, black for cold.)

You can stop a drainpipe leak for years with a

"plumber's poultice." Wrap layers of cloth and wet plaster around the leak. Use strong string to tie the "bandage" in place. Let dry hard before using.

To stop a leaky pipe quickly (but temporarily) cover the hole with plenty of black tape. Or clamp a split hose over the source of the leak. Or clamp on a length of inner tube and a curved metal plate.

Leaking pipe joints can often be repaired, without taking the pipe apart, by smearing the joint with any of several prepared pipe cements, which cost very little and are for sale at hardware stores.

When drainpipes are badly clogged they may need "the full treatment." For this, rent a full-size plumber's snake and probe it all the way through. Simply poking down the drain with a stiff wire will only nudge nearby pieces.

To prevent stoppage in your drainpipes, avoid letting grease go down the drain. It's a good idea always to run hot water down your drain for a few minutes after you do the dishes. Be sure, too, to clean the lint in your washing-machine trap before it gets into the drain. As a headache preventive, give your drain the lye treatment every six months or so.

Infrared lamp does plumbing job. If your sink trap clogs, especially when it's because of too greasy waste, turn your infrared lamp on the pipes. This will start things moving. A commercial drain cleaner will finish the job.

Silence that embarrassing bathroom flush by installing one of the silent valves now available. These replace the old-style rubber bulbs and muffle the sound of flushing.

Hard water will ruin your pipes and cooking utensils more quickly than you may realize. A few dollars a month rents a water softener, complete with the necessary chemicals. In addition to preventing the collection of sludge in your pipes and pots and pans, it will make

This is no problem, of course, when you buy chops or frankfurters. You simply count noses. But other meats washing yourself, your dishes, and your clothes lots easier and pleasanter.

To keep pipes from freezing, don't leave windows open during the winter near uninsulated pipes. Take the time and trouble to wrap all exposed pipes with insulation made for the purpose. Drain all exposed valves through the little valve drain holes in their sides.

Quick rescue for frozen pipes. Too much heat will make frozen pipes burst because heat makes the ice inside the pipe expand. To thaw properly, fill bucket with very hot water and put heavy cloths in it. Wring out cloths and wrap around the pipes. As soon as cloths chill, reheat them and reapply.

ELECTRICAL REPAIRS

Put your house in a new light. If light outlets are poorly placed or insufficient, invest in a good wiring job to assure adequate, more comfortable lighting. You'll cut down eyestrain for whole family and the rooms will look better.

A bad fuse may look good. When the "juice" goes off and you can't find a blown fuse, try replacing the fuses one by one. A fuse may go bad without showing it.

Give yourself time. Install time-delay switches to permit you to walk out of the garage or hall with the lights still on. These switches will automatically turn the lights off for you a few moments after you have snapped them.

To replace a defective wall switch, turn off the main power switch and remove the plate by loosening the plate screw or screws. Then loosen the switch by removing the screws that are set into the box at the sides of the switch. Pull the switch out gently, back of the bolts holding the wires. Install the new switch by replacing these wires under the new screw heads. Now tighten and replace switch and plate.

If your flourescent tube keeps flickering, it's time for a change. You have either the wrong tube for the fixture or the wrong starter. Check and replace.

If your flourescent light gets dark at one end, reverse the tube. This often corrects the fault.

WINDOWS

Windows stick? Paint the window slides with no-polishing floor wax or rub them down with the end of a candle. Tight windows are sometimes caused also by the divider moving out of place. To fix easily, rap the divider to one side.

When a window gets stuck, try running a knife around all the joints. No? Try tapping the window edges with your fist. No? Try using a pry bar on the outside of the window.

Rotted window seals can be repaired by covering decayed parts with aluminum sheeting or corners made of plywood. One piece should cover the top, another the side. Nail fast. When plywood is used, seal the edges with varnish.

Petroleum jelly opens windows. Once a year take this precaution against hard-to-budge windows: Dip a small brush in Vaseline and "paint" the ointment on casing and parting strips of windows. If windows have become stuck, pry open from outside by inserting wedge or chisel under the sash. Before prying up, grease sash runners with Vaseline.

No need to remove the window trim when you have to replace a sash-weight rope. Simply open the little trap door in the side of the slide. Loosen the screw you see there. Now use the old rope or a length of wire through which to feed the new rope. (Use sash chain for minimum trouble.)

Loose windowpanes will rattle in the wind, admit cold air, and eventually break. Save a lot of heat, fuel, and trouble by puttying all loose windows at the first rattle.

A cracked pane of glass can be temporarily held together and weather-proofed with a coat of fresh white shellac on the inside. Vision won't be obstructed by the shellac coat. Breezes and rain will be kept out until the pane is replaced.

To cut glass straight and easy, wipe clean the path of the cutter on the glass, then paint this line with turpentine or any thin oil.

Wax crayons aid glass cutting. Make heavy marks on the glass with wax crayon. Wax will hold your ruler or straight-edge in place as you cut.

SCREENS

Small holes in window screens can be patched by using a few drops of fast-drying model-airplane cement. Larger holes can be repaired by cutting a patch from a discarded screen and gluing it in place.

Use a vacuum cleaner on window screens to remove dust thoroughly and easily. If you haven't the canister-type of vacuum turn your upright machine on its back and run the screen over its mouth.

Weak or broken screen corners can be repaired by using angle-iron mending plates and long wooden screws driven through the corners.

The fastest way to paint a screen is to use a rag or a paint roller. First clean each screen thoroughly, then place it flat so that the paint won't run while drying.

Magic privacy trick. To fix screens so that you can see out without passers-by seeing in, use white paint thinned with turpentine.

Be sure screens fit tight. If window screens are a bit loose, tack weatherstripping along the edges that fit loosely in the window frame. Then you'll be sure to keep out undesirable insects, flying leaves, etc.

29

Heating the Home

A home heating plant powered by natural gas, oil, or electricity delivers heat quickly when it's needed—a desirable feature on chilly fall and spring mornings. Gas and electric heat are also clean and non-polluting. These advantages should be weighed against the rising costs of fuel and electricity and the possibility of fuel shortages.

An electric furnace needs no chimney, and requires no maintenance except for the fan, motor, and filters.

For health and economy, your thermostat should be set during the day between 70° and 72° F., normal indoor temperatures throughout the winter. An overheated house saps your strength, wastes fuel and money.

Raise humidity, not temperature, if house seems chilly at 72° F. Don't raise temperature; that just increases fuel cost unnecessarily. Inexpensive automatic humidifiers or water pans placed on or near radiators will correct the trouble.

When to turn thermostat down:

1. If windows are open for any length of time, while airing rooms during house cleaning.

2. When you go to bed.

3. If room in which thermostat is located is closed off for airing, in order to prevent rest of house from overheating.

Set it at 68°? F. You'll cut your fuel bills by as much as 15 per cent if you select that healthful indoor temperature instead of one only 5 degrees higher.

So you've added a basement rumpus room? Have you checked to make sure your heating unit is still adequate? Whenever you add a room or convert house space to new uses, check on this. You may be putting your present unit to extra strain, thus cutting its efficiency. Also, if you have cut off a room, you may need less heating.

HOW TO CUT HEATING COSTS

Close off a room that's seldom used and don't heat it. Such a room must be sealed off well, however, to keep the cold air in and the hot air from seeping into it. It's a good idea to close off the room in the house that is hardest to heat. Be sure, however, to drain off water in any pipes in the outside walls of unheated rooms or they may freeze, even burst. In extreme weather allow some heat in closed-off rooms to protect the paper and plaster.

The attic doesn't need warmth. Close doors leading to the attic to keep the burner from working overtime. The warm air rises, can escape up the stairs and keep the warmth from where it is needed most.

If your basement isn't heated you'll have cold floors and resulting cold feet in first-floor rooms. For maximum warmth, finish off basement with a full ceiling.

Don't overheat garage. Antifreeze is cheaper than coal. If you do heat the garage, keep it down to 40° F. It's better for your car, better for your pocketbook.

Pull down the shades at dusk and leave them down overnight. This saves fuel and gives you desired nighttime privacy as well. Fuel is saved because the shade partially insulates the window. (In the summertime drawn shades help keep your home cool.)

Rugs and furniture can cause fuel waste if placed where they block radiators or registers.

If you are away from home for some time, during winter, set thermostat down to minimum nighttime temperature of about 55° F. Never turn burner off entirely, because sudden drop in temperature might cause pipes to freeze. Besides, it costs more to bring temperature back up to normal after the thermostat has been turned off and heater idle than to bring it up from lower temperature.

FIREPLACES

Use your fireplace. It not only makes a room cozy in winter but raises the temperature in the room by as much as 10 per cent, especially if coal is burned in the fireplace. When fire is dead and fireplace has cooled, remember to close the damper tight, as it should be when the fireplace is not in use.

Much, in fact, most of the heat in a fireplace goes up the chimney, but there are now available some methods of getting more heat into the room. One type is built into the fireplace itself, with interior vents that circulate the hot air into the room. The other method involves fans attached to special grates and these direct more of the hot air into the room. If you intend to make regular use of your fireplace you might consider some such device.

A piece of asbestos board placed over the fireplace opening saves the heat should you retire before a fire is completely burned out.

Close fireplace dampers when not in use. If dampers are missing and the fireplace isn't used, close the chimney opening.

All fireplaces are safer if protected with a screen.

FIGHTING BACK AT HARD WINTERS

Check list for winterizing your home. Remove screens, then repair, paint and store them flat. Clean window frames, metal screen hangers, and paint. Fit storm windows and doors. Calk around all windows and door frames. Sweep out eavestroughs and give inside a coating of protective paint. Scrape out sidewalk cracks and fill with cement mortar. Insulate exposed plumbing pipes that might freeze. Insulate warm-air ducts and furnace jacket. Get a supply of fuses and store near fuse box.

Cut fuel bills 8 to 20 per cent. Cracks and crevices around doors and windows cost you a lot in wasted heat. The best weather stripping is a metal strip built right into the window sash or door. A less expensive type can easily be put on without special tools. The commonest and by far the cheapest type is felt stripping, and anyone can put it on.

Stop drafts in the house and it will be less costly to heat. Calk door frames and window frames with wood putty compounds. Cover mail slots and door buttons with strips of old leather or beaver board.

Spend once for years of savings. Install storm doors and windows during heating season; be sure doors and windows are adequately equipped with weather stripping. These insulation methods keep the house more comfortable and heating costs down. On stone construction or metal casement windows have the space around the window frames calked to prevent heat leakage.

Those wasteful windows. Engineers figure that glass lets heat escape four times as fast as ordinary uninsulated wall space. The best heat-savers you can get are storm windows and doors that give you a "dead-air" pocket between themselves and your regular windows and doors. This reduces heat loss by as much as two thirds. Experts figure they can easily save you up to 25 per cent in fuel bills.

Insulation means heating thrift. Insulate the hot-water tank and pipes that carry the heat through the house. The materials cost little and mean year-round economy as well as constant hot-water supply and a cooler cellar in summer.

MAINTAINING THE HEATING PLANT

Unless you're a heating expert, don't attempt repairs to heating units yourself. It's better economy to call in a qualified service man.

"Preventive medicine" for heating units. Just as you need an annual check-up by your doctor, so your furnace and boiler should be checked and cleaned once a year by a heating expert. Summertime is best. Have excess soot and scale removed; keep heating costs down. Additional summer treatment: leave furnace doors ajar for free air circulation through firebox. Inexpensive "patch jobs" can be done with putty.

Twin symbols of furnace-fuel waste are black smoke and very hot chimney gases. They're a fire hazard too. Call in your service man if your heating plant doesn't function with at least 70 to 75 per cent efficiency and economy. A trained fuel supplier will give you the efficiency and economical service your heating system requires.

Preventing chimney loss. The greatest waste in home heat is up the chimney. You automatically reduce this loss by keeping the turn damper (the disk-shaped damper in the smoke pipe) as nearly closed as possible. To find the just-right setting for the turn damper, first move the handle $\frac{1}{16}$ of an inch toward the closed position. If the fire continues to burn freely, close the damper still more. Repeat this until the damper is as nearly closed as possible without keeping the fire from burning freely. This will give you the most heat and the least waste of money taking off through the chimney.

Control the draft and save. During heat combustion certain waste materials are formed. These are eliminated by "draft" through the furnace smoke pipe, flue, and chimney. Keep draft passage clear and working well to prevent needless fuel waste. Best solution: have automatic stack-draft control installed.

Install a heat regulator for automatically controlled heat. It saves you steps and money at the same time you keep your home at a desired even temperature.

The nail test. To test the smoke pipe of your home heating plant for weak spots, jab the surface lightly with a heavy nail. If the point penetrates the pipe surface, repair is needed. If only a small section is weak, standard-size, low-priced pipe sections are available at the hardware store. Make the test before the heating season starts. You'll save time, discomfort, higher repair costs, and possible danger of fire.

Your basement runs a temperature? Check your furnace; it it's hot, too, call a service man. Danger signals are browned warm-air ducts and scorched floor joints over the heater.

False economy. Don't connect two heaters to the same chimney flue. This retards the draft and causes poor heat. If you have a separate gas water heater, a separate chimney will save you money.

Check the chimney, too, for loose bricks and breaks, especially in the attic.

Chimneys and flues should be cleaned at least once a year. If the services of a chimney sweep are not available, they can be cleaned by mechanical methods in preference to chemical.

Put several bricks in a burlap bag. Attach bag firmly to strong cord. Working from the top of the chimney, move up and down until soot is removed. Since you need two hands for this, use an extension ladder and hook your leg around a rung.

STEAM AND HOT-WATER SYSTEMS

On steam and hot-water systems, check water for scale and dirt and drain off if necessary. Refill boiler with clean water.

"Pitching" the pipes. Check "pitch" of all steampipes. If incorrectly sloped, they may block heat circulation.

Hot-water and steam boilers should always be equipped with safety valves.

Keep radiators at maximum efficiency. Check vent valves frequently. Open them as often as once a month, if necessary, to let out excess air and assure thorough heat circulation. If valves aren't operating properly, replace them at once.

Radiators give more heat if you place a piece of aluminum foil behind each one. It will reflect more heat back into the room instead of allowing the wall to absorb it.

When radiators go bang! Knock! Wham!!!! Take a look, quick, at the air-vent valves when noisy radiators refuse to get hot. They may be clogged up so that they won't let the cold air out, and if the cold air can't get out, the steam can't get in. Try blowing through the valve to clean it out, or take it off and boil it in a solution of washing soda and water. Defective valves should be replaced, of course.

Try this for knock in radiators. Tilt the radiator slightly downward toward the end at which the steam enters. This permits the water to flow back to the boiler where it belongs. To test the tilt of the radiator, use an ordinary carpenter's level. If it doesn't slope toward the intake end, push a thin wooden wedge under the other end.

If a hot-water radiator won't "hotten," the trouble may come from air trapped in the radiator. Let the trapped air out by using the key provided for opening the radiator. This may take some time, perhaps as much as a half hour, in a house that has been unheated through the summer. Close the key when water squirts out, and stay out of its path because it may be very hot.

To clean out a gummed-up vent, soak it overnight in a grease solvent that will often let the cold air out, while keeping the steam in. Turn off the steam at the valve before removing. If, after cleaning, your radiator still has cold spots, better get a new vent.

If the main valve leaks, remove the handle, loosen and remove the large nut, use a metal pick to remove the old packing, and replace with new. It's O.K. to have the heat on while you do this.

OIL BURNERS

Oil burner won't start? Check the setting of the thermostat. It must be five degrees higher than the thermometer reading or it won't start. Give it a tap, on the chance that it may be merely dust-filled. Check the burner fuse. Check for oil. Check the water gauge, because lack of water will shut off some set-ups.

Why the fuel tank should be full, even during summer months. It prevents the tank from "breathing and sweating" (caused by water condensation), accumulation of wasteful dirt and dust, avoids needless repair expenses. Exterior underground tanks left empty during a heavy summer rain tend to "float" to the surface. Economy tip: Remember, fuel prices usually are lower in summer than during the heating season; another reason for filling tanks at that time.

The right fuel saves money. A grade that's too heavy may cause excess smoke and soot; if too light, it will usually increase your fuel costs. Let a qualified heating man advise you.

Those bargain-price fuels are often of such cheap quality that they cost you more in the long run by giving less heat, causing lowered efficiency of heating unit, etc. It pays to buy fuel from a reputable, reliable source.

30

Safety at Home

HINTS FOR AVOIDING ACCIDENTS AT MAJOR TROUBLE SPOTS AROUND THE HOME

The basic rule for the home handyman is "safety first." Otherwise all the pleasure and profits are of no account. Every tool and material has potential dangers, but if you follow the instructions there should be no problems.

HOW TO PREVENT FIRES

Home fire losses are higher than they should be, in spite of educational and engineering work that's done to prevent them. Here are some basic practices to observe and you'll avoid fire losses.

Smokers should be careful when putting out lighted cigarettes and cigars. Smoking in bed should be absolutely taboo.

Matches should be kept away from younger children and should be used with care by older children and adults.

Furnaces, chimneys, and flues should be inspected and cleaned at least once a year.

Use nonflammable dry-cleaning fluids, and only in

well-ventilated rooms. Any other type should not be used inside the house. Gasoline, naphtha, and other flammables should be stored either in the garage or, preferably, in a separate storage building. Use only approved containers.

Combustible waste materials should not be permitted to accumulate in the home, basement, or garage.

Flammable articles such as celluloid and some plastic materials have a low ignition point, burn very rapidly. They should be kept away from flame or heat. Even the heat of a steam radiator may be sufficient to cause ignition.

Rags covered with oil, wax, and paint should be disposed of or kept in approved containers.

Burn trash or rubbish in outdoor fireplaces or metal baskets, away from the house.

When cleaning floors use nonflammable solvents, with the room well ventilated.

A fire alarm could be included in your home with little extra cost and much increase in safety, especially in homes with young children and elderly persons. Alarm bells should ring on the main floor and in each second-floor bedroom.

Fire extinguishers should be placed on each floor, installed between the probable source of flames and the nearest exit. In the basement, place it near the stairs. In the kitchen, near a door. On the second floor, in the hallway near the stairs.

A soda-acid or water-type extinguisher is adequate for ordinary fires of wood, paper, or rubbish.

A foam extinguisher will also handle fires caused by flammable liquids—grease, oil, gasoline, kerosene, and paint.

A small extinguisher of the carbon-tetrachloride type is advisable for fighting electrical fires and is handy for fires resulting from flammable liquids.

A faucet threaded to take the garden hose is also

helpful in fighting fires. Such threaded faucets should be installed in the basement or laundry and outdoors on either side of the house.

TAKE NO CHANCES WITH ELECTRICITY

"Electro-caution" instead of electrocution. It costs you nothing to play safe in caring for electric cords:

1. Watch for signs of wear. Repair or replace worn cords at once.

2. Keep cords away from heat, water, grease.

3. Never handle cords with wet hands. If you must touch a wet cord, protect your hands with a dry cloth or with gloves and wear rubber overshoes or boots.

4. Don't run cords where friction can fray them, especially under rugs, where they may be tripped over, or where weakened insulation might cause fire.

5. Don't let any cord develop a permanent kink. If it must be hung, use two wooden pegs rather than a nail.

6. Never pull on its cord to detach a plug from the wall. This weakens connection between cord and plug. Pull on the body of plug instead.

7. Never use a cord beyond its current-carrying capacity (lamp cord in heating appliance, etc.).

Safety measure for electric cords. To prevent strain on cord when it is pulled from a socket, even though you pull by the plug, wrap rubber tape around the wire, starting close to the end.

Lamp-cord coverings vary in safety. Rayon fabric is least durable, cotton-and-rayon mixture is somewhat better, and solid rubber or plastic is the best.

For safety's sake, avoid permanent use of extension cords.

Bright idea for light bulbs. By joining a light bulb to its socket with Scotch tape you can prevent youngsters from removing the bulb and possibly getting an electric shock.

When lamp or radio is close to electrical outlet there's usually an untidy length of slack wire to create a safety hazard. Wind the cord around a broomstick. Pull the broom away and you have a neat, tight coil of wire that won't be in the way.

A handy spot for storing spare fuses would be a shelf placed near the fuse box itself. Then, when you need to change a fuse in a hurry, there's no confusion or waste of time.

APPLIANCE CARE

Household appliances with exposed gears should have them so enclosed that fingers or clothing will not be caught.

Washer wringers should have guards to prevent fingers from getting into the rolls. The wringer should also have a release device.

Electric fans and heaters should always have metal guards.

Motor-drive appliances should always be stopped when oiling or making repairs.

Defective appliances, switches, and all electrical devices should be repaired promptly.

To avoid danger of overload, additional circuits should be added to take care of electrical apparatus. Major installations should be made by licensed electricians.

AROUND THE HOUSE

Check the danger spots and act quickly. Instead of complaining about dark cellar stairways or leaky drainpipes that create icy spots in winter, do something about them. Give the whole house periodic inspections and take the necessary precautions immediately, instead of waiting until someone gets hurt. Repair materials usually aren't costly; accidents can be very costly.

Safety in home cleaning of furniture, rugs, etc., can

be achieved if plenty of fresh air carries off any dangerous fumes. Work outdoors if possible. Otherwise let in plenty of ventilation from open windows. Fan placed near a window helps too. Never use cleaning fluids in an unventilated basement. The vapors can travel a long distance over the floor to the heating unit and start a fire.

When is a chair a hazard? If you stand on it to reach for something on a shelf. Solution: Every home should have a safety ladder. It pays for itself many times over, in accidents avoided.

Highly polished floors need not cause broken legs. Be sure that scatter rugs, and especially small rugs at the foot of stairways, are lined with nonslip rug material.

Ladder safety hint. When placing a stepladder on a smooth, slippery surface, such as a highly polished floor, have the ladder rest on a piece of asphalt shingle and be sure of a solid grip.

Hammering nails? Save your fingers. Place a small pad of sponge rubber over spot where nail is to go into wood. It anchors the nail, protects wood surface from hammer marks, and can be removed easily just before you drive the nail home.

Get a good grip. Fit rubber tubing over handles of pliers and they'll be easier to handle. Also insulates them for safer use when making electric repairs.

How to prevent kitchen cuts. Keep sharp knives on wood holders, in plain view, instead of among other utensils in a drawer.

Sharp knives are safe knives. Many more knife cuts occur in the kitchen as a result of dull knives slipping than from sharp ones that do their job efficiently and safely.

Never try to open a can when your hands are wet. In fact, never handle implements with cutting edge unless hands are dry.

When a glass shatters, pick up the pieces with moistened cotton. This will protect your fingers, and even tiniest splinters of glass are caught in the meshes of the cotton.

SOME PRECAUTIONS WITH GAS

Unburned gas contains poisonous carbon monoxide. Care must be taken so flames on ranges don't extinguish by drafts, liquids boiling over, or other mishaps.

Never sleep in a room where gas is used unless there is good ventilation.

If you smell gas, check the valves. If they're closed, it's best to shut the main valve and call the gas company. The windows should always be opened.

To locate a leak in a gas pipe, brush pipe with thick suds. If hole is present, escaping gas will cause bubbles to form at the leaky spot.

Gas water heaters have safety fuses that blow if the water gets too hot. These can be replaced, but have the gas company check the cause of overheating.

When going on vacation it's best to turn off gas water heaters and turn off your range pilot light if it's not one of the new ones that has electric ignition.

HOME BASEMENTS

Stairs should have handrails and should be well lighted. Paint the lowest step white for maximum safety.

Avoid storing paints and varnishes near heating plant. Gasoline or other fuels should not be kept in the basement. Store them elsewhere, in safe containers.

Mount appliances on a platform if the floor in the laundry or laundry area tends to be damp. Proper grounding of appliances is important.

Rafters and other woodwork near the heating plant

should be protected by noncombustible material such as asbestos.

Check furnace pipes that lead to the chimney regularly. They should be in good condition and protected from flammable materials by metal or asbestos insulation.

SAFE POWER MOWING

The dangers and precautions in using power lawn mowers apply equally to hand models or sitdown models. But there is at least one particular precaution that must be observed with sitdown mowers: if there is anything more than the mildest slope to the area being mowed, do not attempt to move parallel to this slope but mow up and down it. And in general, take every precaution possible to avoid tipping a sitdown mower.

Inspect the lawn to be mowed and clear it of stones, wire, or debris. This protects the mower as well as the operator.

Shoo children and pets before you run your power mower. And don't let them play around the mower even when it's not running.

Stop the motor before you work on it, adjusting its performance or removing objects.

Make sure you know how to disengage the clutch quickly in case of emergencies.

Never leave a mower with its motor running for even the briefest moment.

With hand mowers, be especially sure of the terrain: don't let the machine pull you off balance.

Don't smoke when refilling the mower with fuel, and turn the motor off.

It is advisable not to mow wet grass, both for safety's sake and the proper functioning of the mower.

31

Car Conservation

ADD YEARS AND ENJOYMENT,
REDUCE COSTS AND
HEADACHES, BY FOLLOWING
THESE BASICS OF CAR
MAINTENANCE

The modern automobile becomes more sophisticated year by year, and care and maintenance of the more complex parts and systems must now be left to professionals. But the basics of car checkups can still be performed by anyone capable of driving a car. In the case of the most fundamental maintenance, in fact, only the owner-driver can really be responsible.

People often tend to become careless about the basics. Using the car day after day, they take it for granted. One of the best ways to break this pattern of neglect is to take any longer trip as the occasion for a full inspection and some preventive maintenance by the owner-driver. This has a double advantage. Assuming your longer-than-usual trip is going to put some extra strain on the car, it may assure that you don't end up with a breakdown miles from help. And it is a way of performing all those little checkups you have been neglecting.

BASIC MAINTENANCE

Check all lights. Headlights (bright and dim), tail lights, brake lights, turn signals (front and rear), backup lights, and license-plate light. If any don't work, replace or repair them as necessary.

Inspect the wiper blades. The rubber shouldn't be dried or cracked, and the wiper arms shouldn't be bent. Replace if necessary.

To check wiping action, spray the windshield with a garden hose, or if no garden hose is available, take a bucket of water and throw it on the windshield. Then turn the wipers on. You can tell after the wiper blades make a couple of sweeps across the windshield whether they streak or smear.

Make sure the windshield washer is full of fluid. And make sure it works. If you're traveling where the temperature will be below freezing, make sure you use windshield fluid with antifreeze added. Pure water may freeze in the lines. Never use the antifreeze intended for your engine's cooling system to make your own windshield solvent. Use only windshield antifreeze.

Check your brakes if car tends to pull to the left or right. Check both front brakes, not just the one on the side toward which the car pulls.

Look for tire wear. Worn tires can cause an accident. And that's the last thing you want. To check tread wear, stick a penny between the treads, with the top of Mr. Lincoln's head pointed toward the tire. If the tire tread doesn't reach the top of his head, replace the tires—the tread is worn down too much for safety.

Don't forget the spare tire. It's embarrassing to replace one flat tire with another one. Check to make sure the spare's inflated and that it has a decent amount of tread left.

Check the jack, too. You can't change a flat tire if the jack is missing or inoperative. Make sure all the parts are there, and jack the car up just to make sure the jack works.

Open the hood. Check all the fluid levels: brake master-cylinder, power steering pump reservoir (if you have power steering), engine oil, and automatic transmission. Check the automatic transmission fluid level when the engine is warm; otherwise you may get a false reading.

Check the fluid level in the battery and add distilled water if needed. The fluid should reach the bottom of the filler neck in each cell. Although distilled water is best, you can use tap water if distilled water isn't available.

Coolant system should also be checked—preferably every time you fill up with gas. Your car may or may not have a coolant reservoir. If it does, you do not have to worry about steam coming out in your face when you go to add coolant. But if there is no reservoir, you should try to check the coolant only when the engine is cold. If you must remove the radiator cap when the engine is hot, cover the cap with rags to keep from burning your hand. Press down on the cap and turn it counterclockwise until you feel a "click" (about ¼ of a turn). Gradually release your downward pressure on the cap and allow the cooling system pressure to release. When the hissing completely stops, then finish removing the cap. (On some caps there's a little lever you can pull up to release pressure before you twist the cap.)

Trouble's abrewing if you look under the hood and see worn or frayed wiring. Have something done about this at once by your garage mechanic.

Look at all the belts. They should have proper tension and not exhibit wear. To check for wear inspect the edges of each belt and the V part of the belt that fits in the pulleys. Belts shouldn't be frayed, cracked, or glazed. Replace any that are. A loose belt can contribute to decreased engine performance, and a worn belt that breaks can cause all kinds of problems, from a discharged battery to leaving you stranded in the country.

To check belt tension—grasp the belt midway between two pulleys with your thumb and forefinger. Pull up and push down on the belt. If you can deflect it more than half an inch, it's too loose. Loosen the appropriate pulley and take up the slack until you can deflect the belt about half an inch.

Check the heater and radiator hoses. Hoses shouldn't be brittle or cracked. And all clamps should be tight. As a rule of thumb, all hoses should be replaced every two years. If you're going on a long trip and the hoses have been in your car more than two years, don't even bother to inspect them. Replace them with new ones. And unless the clamps are reusable screw clamps, replace the clamps too. Keep hosing, as well as wiring, as far from hot engine parts as possible.

Keep an eye on the oil level if you would spare yourself the cost and torture of burned-out bearings.

Remove the top of the air cleaner and inspect the air filter element. Hold the filter element up to the light. You should be able to see the light through it. If it's blocked and dirty, replace it. A clogged air filter cuts down on engine performance and gas mileage, and in general does nothing good for your engine.

Crawl under the car. Make sure nothing is loose or hanging down, such as part of your exhaust system. If you see anything either underneath, or elsewhere, that you're in doubt about, run your car over to your local service station and get a professional opinion.

Leave nothing to chance. If your car is overdue for a tuneup, oil change, grease job, brake inspection, or wheel bearing repacking, have these services performed.

Put together a "trouble kit." Include in the kit a couple of road flares, a flat-tipped screwdriver, a Phillips-head screwdriver, an adjustable wrench, a single-edge razor blade or sharp knife, some electrical tape, and some wire. It's also a good idea to take along an empty container than can be used for carrying gas or water, plus a funnel to make pouring easier.

TIPS ON FUEL SAVINGS

Have tuneups performed at intervals recommended in owner's manual. This assures maximum engine performance, best mileage, and longer engine life.

When starting, it's important to have the engine catch the first time you step on the starter. Why? Because restarting consumes fuel needlessly. Five false starts, for instance, will eat up as much as two miles of normal driving. Before stepping on the starter, therefore, prepare the engine by pumping the accelerator a couple of times to charge the intake system with fuel—unless your car's direction manual says otherwise.

Change oil regularly. Spending a little here can save a lot in terms of added power, better gasoline mileage, longer bearing life, and many other less tangible results.

Excessive oil consumption can sometimes be traced to an overzealous gas-station attendant who fills the crankcase above the recommended level. Always keep the oil between the "add oil" and "full" marks, not above and not below.

If the clutch slips, have it checked. A slipping clutch robs the engine of power and uses gasoline needlessly.

If your automatic transmission acts up, take your car to a mechanic at once. Correcting the failure is a job for factory-trained experts.

Make sure your automatic choke is working correctly. A malfunctioning choke decreases engine performance and can waste a lot of gas.

At all times start, drive, and stop smoothly. Fast acceleration at any time wastes gas. So does pumping on the acceleraor when waiting at a traffic light. And so, believe it or not, does hard braking, because it means that you have used fuel needlessly to build up too high a speed for the conditions under which you're driving.

Moderate speed consumes much less gas per mile than high speed.

Proper engine heat is important. If the engine is cold, a rich mixture is needed, and a rich mixture burns more gasoline than a lean one. Consequently you should have your thermostat repaired or replaced when the engine runs colder than usual.

A weak spark plug may prevent complete combustion of the fuel. To prevent this, have spark plugs, distributor, battery, ignition coil, wiring, and connections checked regularly.

Incorrect ignition timing, too, can cause fuel to be wasted by making the spark occur at the wrong moment. You should, therefore, have the timing checked at least twice a year.

The carburetor can waste gas by providing too rich a mixture. So have the carburetor and fuel pump adjusted either twice a year or every 5,000 miles, and keep the air filter clean.

Sticking valves, those that are warped and do not seat properly or have excessive carbon deposits, cause "pinging" and loss of compression and thereby waste fuel. This is overcome by having the valves ground and the carbon removed.

Worn piston rings should be replaced because they also cause loss of compression and allow valuable gasoline to escape unburned.

HOW TO GET MORE MILEAGE FROM YOUR TIRES

Keep tires properly inflated. If 30 pounds of pressure is recommended, don't drive around on 24 pounds unless you want to cut life by at least 20 per cent. See that each tire has a valve cap and that the cap is screwed on tight. Never drive on a flat.

Eliminate jack-rabbit starts and avoid screeching stops if you'd like to get full use from your tires. One 10-foot skid can burn off enough tread to reduce tire life by 20 miles or more.

Moderate speed is much more beneficial to tires than high speed, especially around curves, where high speed can multiply tire wear by as much as ten times.

Steer clear of obstructions such as curbs, holes, and rocks in the road. These can greatly shorten tire life by crushing the tire fabric against the rim, snapping cords within the tire, or cutting or bruising the sidewall.

Examine tires once a week for cuts and embedded nails or glass. Even small cuts tend to grow deeper with the passage of time. And they provide a means of entrance for dirt and water, which will eventually destroy the cord structure.

Rotate wheels (including spare) from one hub to another twice yearly, to insure even tread wear and thus increase tire life. After 5 switches each tire will have been in use on each hub and will also have been temporarily retired to the trunk for a spare-tire rest.

Have wheel alignment, wheel balance, and steering-wheel-play checked once a year. Misaligned wheels can decrease tire life by $1/4$ to $1/2$; out-of-balance wheels will shimmy and cause tires to wear unevenly; and too much play in the steering wheel will let wheels weave back and forth, producing spotty tread wear.

Wheel balancing calls for special skill. Beware the mechanic who installs many balance weights. He may be trying to correct his own mistakes.

BATTERY CARE

Inspect the terminal connections of the battery if it won't hold a charge. To avoid corrosion, the terminals should be kept clean and bright.

Corrosion can be prevented by covering the terminals with petroleum jelly (Vaseline). If corrosion has already set in, disconnect the terminals from their posts and clean both the terminals and the posts with a solution of water and baking soda. Make sure everything is thoroughly dry before putting the terminals back in place.

Unless you drive several miles every day, the alternator may not keep the battery charged. If you don't drive regularly, have the battery checked often and recharged when necessary.

When you lay the car up for any length of time, have your garage mechanic remove the battery and connect it to the garage's trickle charger. This is also known as standby charging or set storage. It will guarantee that the battery won't be dead when you want to recommission your car.

HINTS FOR HARD WINTERS

If it's extremely cold, have your mechanic change the spark plugs for ones a step higher in heat range, to prevent fouling while the choke is in operation.

Car hard to start? If may be running too cold because antifreeze makes the engine operate at a lower temperature than it does with tap water. A winter-range thermostat will overcome this.

When stuck in deep snow or ruts, with no chains available, let most of the air out of the rear tires. This increases traction enough to allow you to pull out. Then drive very slowly (to prevent damage to tires and rims) to the nearest service station and pump the tires back up again.

On ice or in snow, drive with no sudden throttle changes, no jazzing of the accelerator, no panicky lead-footing or braking. Instead maintain a moderate, steady speed, using the engine to brake as well as to accelerate.

Power brakes may cause the wheels to lock and skid. To prevent this, always dab at the pedal rather than apply a steady pressure. This is especially true in winter driving.

Proper following distance is even more important in snow than it is on clear, dry roads; so increase the distance between your car and the one ahead from one car length per 10 miles per hour to several car lengths.

During the winter keep the battery completely charged. A partly charged battery can freeze at 20° F. and a discharged battery can freeze at 32° F. Nine times out of 10 a frozen battery has had it, can't be resuscitated.

Even a well-charged battery may not prove sufficient when it is a matter of starting a car that has sat for any length of time in truly frigid weather. There are, of course, electrical device to keep the whole motor warm. But one trick that might be used by anyone expecting an exceptionally cold spell is to bring the battery in and place it by the furnace. Just be sure to fasten the cables firmly to the terminal and you should get full power from your battery through the coldest weather.

Don't use heavy oil in cold weather. The needless friction it causes can be conquered only by using extra fuel.

Put a can of gas-line antifreeze in the fuel tank at every fillup to prevent gas line freezeup.

For a frozen lock, heat the key with a match or cigarette lighter before inserting it in the lock. The hot key usually melts the ice in the lock in about 30 seconds or so. Reheat the key as necessary.

The tables below are set up to help you convert units commonly used when driving a car. The answers

you arrive at will be approximate, but accurate enough
for nonscientific purposes.

WHEN YOU KNOW THE U.S. UNIT	MULTIPLY BY:	TO FIND THE METRIC UNIT
Miles	1.6	Kilometers
Gallons	3.8	Liters
Miles per gallon	0.42	Kilometers per liter

WHEN YOU KNOW THE METRIC UNIT	MULTIPLY BY:	TO FIND THE U.S. UNIT
Kilometers	0.62	Miles
Liters	0.26	Gallons
Kilometers per liter	2.4	Miles per gallon

Index

25¢OFF

25¢OFF

25¢ OFF

ATTENTION CONSUMERS: Do not ask your retailer to honor this coupon unless you make the required purchase. Any other use constitutes FRAUD on your part. You must pay any sales tax on your purchase. **OFFER EXPIRES DECEMBER 31, 1982.**

ATTENTION RETAILER: Subject to your compliance as required herein for each coupon you properly accept as our authorized agent we will pay you 7¢ plus the face value of the coupon or your documentable retail price on coupons for free goods. Coupons will be honored when presented by retail distributors of our merchandise or associations or clearing houses, approved by us, acting for and at the sole risk of our retailers. It is FRAUD to present coupons for redemption other than as provided herein and without INVOICES in your possession which must be furnished to us on request to prove your purchase of sufficient stock to cover submitted coupons. Mailing of coupons which have not been legitimately received from consumers could bring prosecution under FEDERAL U.S. MAIL STATUTES. We reserve the right to withhold payment on any shipment of coupons when the terms of this offer have not been complied with on all coupons submitted and, to confiscate the coupons. This coupon may not be assigned or reproduced and is redeemable only on the specified product(s). Coupons not forwarded within six months from the expiration date below will not be honored. **OFFER EXPIRES DECEMBER 31, 1982.** Vicks Health Care Division, Richardson-Vicks Inc., P.O. Box 1336, Clinton, Iowa 52734. Cash value 1/20 of 1¢ - Limit One Coupon Per Purchase.

25¢ OFF

ATTENTION CONSUMERS: Do not ask your retailer to honor this coupon unless you make the required purchase. Any other use constitutes FRAUD on your part. You must pay any sales tax on your purchase. **OFFER EXPIRES DECEMBER 31, 1982.**

ATTENTION RETAILER: Subject to your compliance as required herein for each coupon you properly accept as our authorized agent we will pay you 7¢ plus the face value of the coupon or your documentable retail price on coupons for free goods. Coupons will be honored when presented by retail distributors of our merchandise or associations or clearing houses, approved by us, acting for and at the sole risk of our retailers. It is FRAUD to present coupons for redemption other than as provided herein and without INVOICES in your possession which must be furnished to us on request to prove your purchase of sufficient stock to cover submitted coupons. Mailing of coupons which have not been legitimately received from consumers could bring prosecution under FEDERAL U.S. MAIL STATUTES. We reserve the right to withhold payment on any shipment of coupons when the terms of this offer have not been complied with on all coupons submitted and, to confiscate the coupons. This coupon may not be assigned or reproduced and is redeemable only on the specified product(s). Coupons not forwarded within six months from the expiration date below will not be honored. **OFFER EXPIRES DECEMBER 31, 1982.** Vicks Health Care Division, Richardson-Vicks Inc., P.O. Box 1336, Clinton, Iowa 52734. Cash value 1/20 of 1¢ - Limit One Coupon Per Purchase.

25¢OFF

ATTENTION CONSUMERS: Do not ask your retailer to honor this coupon unless you make the required purchase Any other use constitutes FRAUD on your part. You must pay any sales tax on your purchase. **OFFER EXPIRES DECEMBER 31, 1982.**

ATTENTION RETAILER: Subject to your compliance as required herein for each coupon you properly accept as our authorized agent we will pay you 7¢ plus the face value of the coupon or your documentable retail price on coupons for free goods Coupons will be honored when presented by retail distributors of our merchandise or associations or clearing houses, approved by us, acting for and at the sole risk of our retailers. It is FRAUD to present coupons for redemption other than as provided herein and without INVOICES in your possession which must be furnished to us on request to prove your purchase of sufficient stock to cover submitted coupons Mailing of coupons which have not been legitimately received from consumers could bring prosecution under FEDERAL U.S. MAIL STATUTES We reserve the right to withhold payment on any shipment of coupons when the terms of this offer have not been complied with on all coupons submitted and, to confiscate the coupons This coupon may not be assigned or reproduced and is redeemable only on the specified product(s). Coupons not forwarded within six months from the expiration date below will not be honored.

OFFER EXPIRES DECEMBER 31, 1982. Vicks Health Care Division, Richardson-Vicks Inc., P.O. Box 1336, Clinton, Iowa 52734. Cash value 1/20 of 1¢ - **Limit One Coupon Per Purchase.**

25¢OFF

ATTENTION CONSUMERS: Do not ask your retailer to honor this coupon unless you make the required purchase Any other use constitutes FRAUD on your part. You must pay any sales tax on your purchase. **OFFER EXPIRES DECEMBER 31, 1982.**

ATTENTION RETAILER: Subject to your compliance as required herein for each coupon you properly accept as our authorized agent we will pay you 7¢ plus the face value of the coupon or your documentable retail price on coupons for free goods. Coupons will be honored when presented by retail distributors of our merchandise or associations or clearing houses, approved by us, acting for and at the sole risk of our retailers. It is FRAUD to present coupons for redemption other than as provided herein and without INVOICES in your possession which must be furnished to us on request to prove your purchase of sufficient stock to cover submitted coupons Mailing of coupons which have not been legitimately received from consumers could bring prosecution under FEDERAL U.S. MAIL STATUTES We reserve the right to withhold payment on any shipment of coupons when the terms of this offer have not been complied with on all coupons submitted and, to confiscate the coupons This coupon may not be assigned or reproduced and is redeemable only on the specified product(s). Coupons not forwarded within six months from the expiration date below will not be honored.

OFFER EXPIRES DECEMBER 31, 1982. Vicks Health Care Division, Richardson-Vicks Inc., P.O. Box 1336, Clinton, Iowa 52734. Cash value 1/20 of 1¢ - **Limit One Coupon Per Purchase.**

NOTES

NOTES